STOP
THE PARISH
I want to get Off!

AUDREY CARTER

MONARCH
Crowborough

First published 1994

Unless otherwise indicated, biblical quotations are from the Revised
Standard Version

ISBN 1 85424 262 8

British Library Cataloguing in Publication Data
A catalogue record for this book is available
from the British Library.

Production and Printing in England for
MONARCH PUBLICATIONS
Broadway House, The Broadway, Crowborough,
East Sussex TN6 1HQ by
Nuprint Ltd, Harpenden, Herts, AL5 4SE.

To the men in my life

Dear God,
Here is the Eleventh Commandment: remember she is the wife of the rector, not the rector's wife.

Audrey

Saturday 26th August

Dear God,

It's us, the Carter family. You must have heard of us by now because St Jude's Church has been on its knees for a whole year praying for a new incumbent. They've just had an interregnum and it was painful.

When we arrived today, we nearly missed the rectory hidden behind the last bit of true wilderness in Britain. The churchwardens, Major Crabtree and Miss Willis, met us at the gates (one in each hand) and helped us beat a pathway to the front door with their walking sticks and, after applying a bit of 'heave ho', the whole Carter family plus Samuel Smudge, the black Labrador and Pooky the black cat, fell into the Grade II listed, crumbling Georgian refrigerator.

The only floor covering was a year's unsolicited mail in the hall and a notice sticky-taped to the floor at the entrance to the study alerting us to the 2ft x 3ft hole ahead.

Audrey

Sunday 27th August
Fifteenth Sunday after Pentecost
Theme: Those in Authority

Dear God,

There's rising damp and falling plaster and no heating in the five bedrooms and half a bathroom. Major Crabtree assured us that the last rector and his family got by with a few extra jerseys.

Miss Willis apologised for the fourth bedroom. Our predecessor's son had been let loose with tins of red and green high gloss creating a sort of lettuce and tomato salad environment. That is one clergy child who doesn't feel inhibited.

Audrey

PS   Please God, send us some extra jerseys and miracle paint stripper and remind me to clear the mushrooms growing in the corner of our loo before Mother moves into her flat around the corner next week.

Monday 28th August
Augustine, Bishop of Hippo, Teacher of the Faith, c 430

Dear God,

Mrs Next-Door called this morning. Did we need anything and would we please stop Samuel Smudge hurling his 86lbs against the fence every time Bert, their retired greyhound, goes out to do his business?

Tom has just booked his first baptism. 'I want the ruddy baby done,' declared a young woman on the rectory steps this afternoon.

'And before you say anything, Audrey,' said the future Rector of St Jude's to me as he closed the door, 'remember, it's the same Holy Spirit who brought her here today to have her baby "done", that also guided us to St Jude's.'

Audrey

Tuesday 29th August
Beheading of St John the Baptist

Dear God,

Why me? Five years ago I was the wife of a successful business man. I'd never manned a church hall tea urn or run a jumble sale. I had none of the talents a congregation expects in a rector's wife. When I met Tom he was agonising over winning contracts. Now, twenty-five years later, he's agonising over winning souls!

We now live in a diocesan house. Our three sons, Derek, Anthony and Martin who are very enthusiastic about their Dad doing his own thing, don't realise that he has to 'do it' on a much reduced salary; that the Archbishop of Canterbury does not hand out bonuses nor declare dividends, and that fillet of steak is a nice memory. Added to all this God, I don't even know my way around the *Alternative Service Book* yet.

In short God, I'm having difficulty squeezing through the eye of the needle and it's Tom's induction service at St Jude's tomorrow! OH GOD, WHY ME?

Audrey

Wednesday 30th August

Dear God,

It's all over. Tom was inducted this evening as the Rector of St Jude's. I am now the wife of the rector; Derek,

Anthony and Martin are the rector's sons; Sammy and Pooky are the rectory dog and cat respectively, and Josephine is the rectory car. I'm still on a spiritual high God; it was all so uplifting and awe inspiring.

I arrived at St Jude's after Tom with Mother and the boys. The ushers at the door parted like the Red Sea when they realised who we were, and three of them led us a hundred miles down the centre aisle to the left front pew.

A hush closed in behind us as the congregation realised they were looking at their new rector's family and Martin, with a quick 360° swivel of his head, was able to report that about four hundred pairs of eyes were boring into our backs.

Mother sent a message along the row to me saying she hoped they had a strong Mothers' Union and did I think she was right to have worn her navy and white.

Then the organ swelled with the opening bars of 'Lo! he comes with cloud descending' and up the aisle came Tom with the bishop, archdeacon, rural dean and clergy from neighbouring parishes, all in their ecclesiastical best. It was quite mind blowing and I had to send down to Mother for a tissue.

The bishop said that we were all priests in the service of God and must all minister to one another; that Tom would bring his own special God-given gifts to his ministry, which would be different to those of his predecessors.

He stressed the need for a priest to have time and space for his own private prayer and meditation, for without spiritually refuelling himself, he would not be able to refresh others.

Finally, after a rousing rendition of 'Be Thou my vision, O Lord of my heart', Tom stepped forward and from the chancel steps gave his first blessing to the congregation of St Jude's.

There followed a blur of faces, names and handshakes and a feast of sandwiches, cup cakes and sausage rolls in the hall, accompanied by a range of disturbing thoughts. How were the boys holding up to all the attention? Were they descending on the food like a plague of locusts? And what was

Mother telling the ladies of St Jude's? Martin located me at one point with the news that Nana was telling them that I'd walked at nine months and was dry by twelve months!

What I needed most of all just then God was to stand next to Tom and feel his hand close over mine, but already he was surrounded by people.

Audrey

Thursday 31st August
1.30am

Dear God,

It's me again; I can't sleep. Oh God, let it all be alright. Help Tom to be a good rector and let St Jude's come to know him as their father in Christ. I don't know what his special gifts are God, except for a wonderful speaking voice and smile. But he's here today because five years ago you put your hand on him.

It's me who needs your help most. Help me to get used to living in someone else's house and sharing Tom with so many other people. Help me to be cheerful about our much reduced income and uncertain financial future. Help me not to miss my own car too much. Help me not to be too sensitive about everything that is said about me and particularly about Tom. Above all, help me to keep my sense of humour. We have come such a long way and even the boys have had to make big adjustments.

Thank you God for always being there to hear about my doubts and fears and for listening tonight, and now I must just nip downstairs. I forgot to take the mincemeat out of the freezer.

Audrey
Wife of the rector.

Thursday 31st August
Aidan, Bishop of Lindisfarne, Missionary, 651
John Bunyan, Author, 1688

Dear God,

Why, oh why, didn't I listen to the bishop's wife at Tom's ordination. 'Don't join anything for the first ten years, my dear,' she'd whispered.

This morning the Enrolling Member of the Mothers' Union phoned. Would I join them next Tuesday when Mrs Tarrington-Jones will be showing a thousand slides of her visit to her daughter in Little Rock, Arkansas, USA, followed by a talk on osteoarthritis?

After lunch the chairman of the Young Families Group dropped by. Would I join them on Wednesday night for a talk on bedwetting?

The captain of the bellringers came at four. Had I any bell-ringing experience? During tea Brenda the Sunday School Supervisor rang. Would I swell their ranks? They needed a teacher for the two to three year olds behind the piano, or the ten to twelve year olds on the stage.

Oh God, I'm not interested in osteoarthritis, I'm too young! I'm not interested in bedwetting, I'm too old! Too late! I've said yes to them all. I feel I've just gone public, swallowed up by the system; like spending a penny in one of those automatic loos.

Audrey

PS   Please God, send me the fact sheet for wives of new rectors and please stop Mother going on about our 'changed circumstances'. She's convinced the rectory kitchen is about to explode.

Friday 1st September
Giles of Provence, Abbot and Confessor, 720

Dear God,

Would you please have a word with St Francis about a
'born again' dog? This morning Samuel Smudge escaped and
marked out his parish boundaries. At lunchtime a Mrs
Barlavington phoned. Sam had had a go at her Bengi who'd
just gone up to say 'hello'; Bengi was only a little puppy dog
and she wouldn't take it further this time, but that if it
happened again. . . .

I haven't been here a week yet God and I'm already
known as the owner of 'that dog'. Together we can clear the
local green of dog walkers in two minutes flat – and what he
doesn't tackle he mounts!

Audrey

PS   What's wrong with a good dog fight now and again
God? It sort of clears the air, like a good thunderstorm.

Saturday 2nd September

Dear God,

Helped Mother move into her flat this morning. While the
boys and I pushed and shoved the furniture, she disappeared
next door to introduce herself as the mother-in-law of St
Jude's new rector.

But the new rector needs help with his first sermon. He's
got as far as emptying people's minds of all the unworthy
thoughts they've brought in with them, but can't find anything worthy for them to take out with them.

Do they really listen? Tom says they'll be too busy craning
their necks to see what the new rector's wife is wearing. But,
even if they don't listen, there's always that visiting student

of theology to be reckoned with, never mind those retired priests in mufti.

Audrey

PS Mother says she doesn't think black suits Tom.

Sunday 3rd September
Sixteenth Sunday after Pentecost
Theme: The Neighbour

Dear God,
   Our first Sunday at St Jude's today. Went early to avoid running the gauntlet of all those eyes again. Mother was already in the front pew wondering if she were right to have worn a hat. Martin arrived late wearing Tom's yachting tie, but Brother Ass had got the better of Anthony and Derek.
   I don't remember much about the service God except praying that Tom wouldn't fall over and deciding that in future I'd just sit anywhere and not so conspicuously in the front row.
   Afterwards there were more handshakes, new faces and smiles. Finally, we were back in the rectory.
   Father Benton, a retired priest in the parish, rang tonight offering his help and enquiring whether Tom had had 'the experience' yet, ie 'the experience of climbing into the pulpit, surveying the flock for the first time and wondering how on earth you're going to realise the Kingdom of God through them'.
   Tom confessed that he didn't remember much about the morning's service except the wonderful cup of coffee in the hall afterwards.

Audrey

Monday 4th September

Dear God,

Martin set fire to the rectory tonight. I can see it now splashed across the billboards at the corner newsagent, in the parish magazine under 'Round and About', headlined in *The Church Times*, reflected upon in *The Tablet* and discussed at Synod–'Rector's Son Burns Down Rectory'.

Martin, who likes things bigger, better and instant, including flames, covered the grate opening with newspaper. The paper caught fire, flew up the chimney, and set alight two hundred years of Grade II listed soot. With a dreadful roar the Georgian chimney turned into a furnace.

Panic set in. Water was thrown into the grate and the cat, the dog and Martin into the garden. Then, three to four minutes into the fire the phone rang. It was Miss Willis. Did we know the rectory was on fire? She'd seen flames coming out of the chimney when she'd stepped outside to find Orion's Belt for her cousin who'd come up from Bognor for a few days ''cause she's just had her stones removed and is feeling a bit poorly'.

We were now six minutes into the fire. I assured her Tom had it all under control, hoped she'd find Orion's Belt, sorry to hear about her cousin's stones, and that I had a cousin in Bognor too.

We were now seven and a half minutes into the fire. Suddenly, physics lessons were remembered. Derek found a board to cover the grate and exclude the air. The roaring stopped, the fire went out, the cat, the dog and Martin let in, and Tom got off his knees.

Audrey

PS   Should I warn the sixth form college that they've got a pyromaniac joining them tomorrow?

Tuesday 5th September

Dear God,
There's a buzz going round the girls in the choir. It's our three sons. How can I warn them that my three, six foot one and one half inch, 22 carat, fully undomesticated offspring are genuine homespun layabouts with endearing characteristics such as:

1) The execution of all jobs, no matter how difficult, with one hand in their pocket.
2) A three mile 'fallout' of coffee mugs and beer cans wherever they go.
3) A dogged determination that dirty clothes belong under the bed.
4) Another dogged determination that sopping wet bath towels belong on the bed (unmade of course).

5) An inability to rinse a teaspoon without getting their feet wet.

6) And an amazing dexterity when depositing rubbish in the dustbin so that all the garbage slithers down between the bin and its liner–and this, remember, with only one hand!

Audrey

PS The girls might not see much of 'The Brothers Karamazov' at St Jude's though God. They suddenly became atheists when Tom was ordained (a sort of self protection), except, that is, when they're writing exams when, as you know, they like their Dad to get on his hotline to you about how hard they've worked. Anyway Anthony starts at the Poly on the 5th October and Derek goes back to university on the 6th, so the sopranos will have to hang on till half term.

Wednesday 6th September

Dear God,

Met Doris Stubbs, chief flower-arranger of St Jude's today. She said Father George, Tom's predecessor, never interfered, gave her a free hand. Said it wasn't an easy job and that people took it for granted, but that they'd notice if they came in and there were no flowers. 'They'd say, "What's happened to Doris Stubbs, is she ill?" 'Cause they like to have something to look at during the long bits when the rector's up there at the high altar doing his own thing'.

She said Father George had depended on her, never took her for granted, always a word of praise and a card at Christmas and chocs at Easter, and that he knew a good flower-arranger when he saw one.

Mother says I must watch Doris Stubbs.

Audrey

Thursday 7th September
Evurtius, Bishop of Orleans

Dear God,

The editor of the parish magazine called to get some copy on 'The Rector's Wife – her enthusiasms and her ambitions.' He came at a bad moment. The chief organiser of The Holy Dusters (St Jude's volunteer cleaning ladies), had been on the phone – would I join them on Friday mornings to clean St Jude's?

'Yes, Mr Magazine Man,' I said, 'but first I'd like to get in touch with myself, find out who I am and what "my own thing" is. Then I think I'd like to learn to tap dance and all that before those men in white coats take me away to a home for bewildered clergy wives.'

I felt much better having got that off my chest and offered him a cup of tea, but he seemed in a frightful hurry.

Audrey

Friday 8th September
The Blessed Virgin Mary

Dear God,

Tom says, now that the boys are just about off my hands, I've got time to find myself. Doesn't he know God that there's a whole congregation out there looking for me too?

Audrey

Saturday 9th September

Dear God,

Mother says that in her day people stayed where they were when they got there. None of this 'changing horses mid-stream', none of this 'finding oneself' and, as for being 'called', there was a large granite building outside the town for those who heard voices.

Audrey

Wednesday 13th September
Cyprian, Bishop of Carthage, Martyr, 258

Dear God,

Just been invaded by the Men's Society. Evidently Father George let them meet in the rectory every second Wednesday in the month because the Townswomen's Guild Bridge Club hires the hall on that evening.

Tom took leave of his senses and mentioned tea and I had to make a dash to Mother's for more milk. Said it was for custard otherwise she'd have hotfooted it round here to help and make it quite clear to the Men's Society that she didn't put me through college to become a mass caterer.

But, I know where I'm going on the second Wednesday of the month–to the Townswomen's Guild Bridge Club!

Audrey

Thursday 14th September
Holy Cross Day

Dear God,

Sammy's disappeared. One minute he was digging up Tom's Spider lilies and the next minute he was gone. We've been scouring the parish all day. It's now 10pm. How can we lock up and go to bed while that poor dog is out there somewhere–lost?

Audrey

Friday 15th September

Dear God,

Rang the police station at 7.30am. Yes, they had a big black Labrador. Would we fetch him straight away as he'd been sitting in the kennel all night howling his eyes out and they were all going deaf.

Evidently he'd made for the local grocer yesterday in pursuit of their resident Jack Russell who's on heat, causing havoc among the sacks of potatoes, the OAPs and the new bread delivery.

The shopkeeper, who couldn't cope with commerce and copulation at the same time, had rung the station.

The charge for his bed and breakfast was 70p and the sergeant said they'd laced his drinking water with copper sulphate.

Tom says he's now got his sermon for Sunday–Love Knows No Bounds.

Audrey

Saturday 16th September

Dear God,

Had my annual wallow tonight and I'm ready to die for England. I've just watched the Last Night of the Proms. Oh God, I love it.

Do you think you could fix it for me to go to a performance? I'm a bit too old to paint my face with the Union Jack, but I'd take the flag I waved at the Queen's Silver Jubilee celebrations.

I too want to stand up and sing 'Land of Hope and Glory', 'Rule Britannia', and most of all, 'Jerusalem'. Of course I'd cry, but I'd be so happy.

Tom said he'd have 'She made it to the Last Night of the Proms' engraved on my tombstone.

Well God, can you fix it for me?

Audrey

Sunday 17th September
Eighteenth Sunday after Pentecost
Theme: The Offering of Life

Dear God,

A new lady appeared in the back pew today clutching a miniature poodle. Bets were rapidly placed by the choir. Would she take it up to the communion rail or leave it in the pew?

She did neither. She took it as far as the front row (at which point the choir went to pieces) and handed it into the safe-keeping of a very surprised Major Crabtree, who was busy controlling the flow of communicants, and then collected it on the way back to her pew.

Audrey

Tuesday 19th September

Dear God,

At 8.30am a band of workmen arrived at the rectory. By evening the hole in the study floor had been repaired, four cracked windows and a length of guttering replaced, the chimney swept and the upstairs measured for heating. I feel my life is coming together.

It was wonderful having so many people assembled at one time making things come right for me. I ran around making numerous cups of tea and coffee, agonising over whether I should give them a mug or a cup and saucer and generally just willing them not to stop!

Audrey

Thursday 21st September
St Matthew the Apostle

Dear God,

The Mothers' Union had a talk on 'Living in South Africa' followed by a discussion. Mrs Heyshott stood up and said that everyone knew she wouldn't hurt a flea, but that she thought that all blacks in England should go back to where they came from.

Mother, recalling her trip to India in 1929, said she was no racist, but give her an African any day rather than an Indian—she couldn't abide them.

Audrey

Monday 25th September
Lancelot Andrewes, Bishop of Winchester, 1626

Dear God,

Tom and I went for a long walk this morning. Near Church Farm we met Doris Stubbs negotiating a stile laden with bunches of wild grasses and hay and three carrier bags of straw. Her preparations for Harvest Festival are obviously well under way.

Audrey

Wednesday 27th September
Ember Day, Vincent de Paul, Founder of Vincentian Order, 1660

Dear God,

The Harvest Festival Supper is over and the last pudding spoon washed up. As fifty percent more tickets were sold

than the hall could comfortably accommodate, Major
Crabtree, fearing that free movement in such circumstances
would only lead to chaos, ran the whole show on boarding
school if not military lines, with HQ sited on the stage.

Once seated no one was allowed to move. Even a visit to
the loo had to be cleared by Wally Burt, the Major's right
hand man.

Two monitors were appointed from each trestle table to
bring the harvest suppers from the kitchen: cling film covered plates of one piece of cold ham, one cold sausage, half a
tomato, two lettuce leaves and a dollop of potato salad.

When this had been consumed a signal came from HQ
and all the dirty plates were passed down the length of the
twenty-five feet long trestle tables, followed by blue plastic
buckets for the dirty knives and forks.

It all made my suggestion to the Harvest Festival Supper
Catering Committee that we go for a relaxed, candlelight
buffet supper between bales of straw seem wildly irrespon-
sible.

Miss Flowers, flushed from a glass of Sainsbury's Rosé,
leaned forward over her apple pie and custard and said, 'I'm
sure God doesn't mind us letting our hair down now and
again.'

When the last pudding spoon had disappeared into the
blue plastic buckets, Major Crabtree auctioned off the two
surplus apple pies followed by the floral arrangements, the
money to be divided between the roof and the organ funds.
We were then instructed to fold up the tablecloths and pass
them down to the end.

Only then were we allowed to stand up and stretch our
legs while the Men's Society dismantled the trestle tables and
manoeuvred the chairs into rows facing the stage for the
traditional Harvest Supper entertainment. This took the
form of community singing punctuated by two solo items
from Doris Stubbs singing, 'We'll Gather Lilacs' and 'Midnight' from *Cats*. Mr Barnes, St Jude's resident poet, followed this with a long poem covering all the main events in

the life at St Jude's since the last Harvest Festival, ending
with:

> The rectory's once more filled with life,
> With a rector, his dog, his cat and his wife.
> And we at St Jude's would just like to say
> We hope you'll like us; we hope you'll stay.

Audrey

PS I've forgiven him for his positioning of 'wife' in the
second line.

Thursday 28th September

Dear God,
  This time next week Derek will be back at university.
He'll be sharing a flat with Kev and Mandy when he returns—
something about being able to concentrate on work more
and having to get away from the noise of the 'absolutely
juvenile first years!' Tom greeted the news with raised eyebrows which said, 'If you believe that you'll believe anything.'
  He's been going through my pan cupboard, cutlery
drawer and linen cupboard like a magpie and today moved
round to Mother's to pick over her bits and pieces.
  It's nothing short of a miracle God how quickly young
minds can be diverted from Foster's lager to egg flips.

Audrey

Saturday 30th September
Ember Day. St Jerome, Priest, Confessor and Doctor, 420

Dear God,

Tom has just come back from St Jude's in quite a state. Doris Stubbs and helpers have been decorating for Harvest Festival tomorrow and he says the altar is as cluttered as a woman's dressing table – loaves of plaited bread, poppies and ears of corn everywhere. He's had to clear a spot for his feet between the pumpkins, bunches of carrots, potatoes and hubbard squash.

There's a pottery mouse peering down from the pulpit between the wheat sheaves and two field mice made from felt chasing each other across the altar frontal. Tom says they'll have to go, but I've persuaded him to keep the one on the pulpit. I was sure you wouldn't mind God. Anyway Doris Stubbs will complain to me, not to Tom or you.

Audrey

Sunday 1st October
Twentieth Sunday after Pentecost
Theme: Endurance

Dear God,

Had a very good turn out this morning. Recognised Mr and Mrs Anderson from Church Farm and Joe the dairyman from The Beeches.

From between the wheat sheaves and the pottery mouse Tom delivered his Harvest Festival sermon to St Jude's. He quoted the English translation of a Latin inscription scratched on the east window of the library at Montacute House. It not only praises the understanding the farmer has of nature but also points to you God in the ordinary.

Happy is the man with the keen intellect and superhuman eagerness to reveal the innermost secrets of nature; happy is he who can grasp the causes and relationships of matter; who can walk in the footsteps of Newton as his companion. But happy too is the man who cares for his fields; who appreciates all the manifold riches of his garden; who has learnt the art of grafting trees that each may thrive in its favourite soil; and who knows which are happiest in the rich mud and ooze of the pond; which rejoice on the rocky ridges; which shun the biting cold of the north wind; and which flower high up in the snowy wastes of Scythia. Do not scorn or grumble about this modest toil; it is shared by the greatest gardner of all. Do not look for Him amid the stars of heaven; for it is in the ordinary things of life that you may find God.

After we'd sung 'We plough the fields and scatter', the bread and wine were taken up followed by the Sunday school with their Harvest Festival offerings, and then by the rest of us with ours.

We ended up with a mountain of windfall apples from local gardens, a good supply of vegetables and a variety of tinned food.

Then my eyes lighted on a small box of Black Magic. Someone, I thought, has imagination. Someone realises that man cannot live on windfall apples and baked beans alone. I could imagine the recipient's surprise finding them under the vegetables and fruit and the pleasure he'd have chomping his way through them.

Audrey

Wednesday 4th October
St Francis of Assisi, Friar, 1226

Dear God,

Our middle son has just discovered 'life abundant'. Last week, armed with his grant cheque he disappeared through the portals of our local bank. Thirty minutes later he re-appeared complete with a Student's Survival Kit and the confident air of a man who's arrived. The past week has gone by in a flash of cheque book and card as he's equipped himself with the bare essentials for student survival.

First came the radio-cum-tape recorder-cum-tea maker, cum-alarm clock, cum-blower of the mind and ear drums—a sort of early warning system. Second came the bottles of assorted pongs in pre-shave, after-shave and in-between shave. Third came the student's supplementary health foods—beer, Cokes, chocolate and chips.

Yesterday he packed his whole wardrobe into four bin bags, took it to OXFAM and on the way home bought a new one. Verily, he has discovered the bottomless bank!

Audrey

Thursday 5th October

Dear God,

Anthony and Derek have gone, Martin's at college, Tom's at a Chapter meeting, the rectory's like a morgue and Sammy's following me around in case I disappear too.

I know that Anthony's Polytech is only a few miles away, and that it was right that he went into residence and didn't commute from home, and that he'll probably be here at weekends for a square meal, but I miss him already.

I wonder how Derek, Kev and Mandy will get on. Will they remember to turn off the gas, switch off the iron, budget for electricity, gas and telephone bills? Will they remember to put out the bin on the right day? I won't phone Derek until his birthday on Saturday God. Can't have Kev and Mandy think his mother's breathing down his neck.

Audrey

Saturday 7th October

Dear God,
   Phoned Derek after breakfast. He was in the middle of a bumper fry up for them all to celebrate his birthday and their new home. Oh God, I know his fry ups and could almost smell the burning fat and see the flames from here. Tom said not to worry; they'll be down to bread and scrape by the end of next week.

Audrey

Sunday 8th October
Twenty-first Sunday after Pentecost
Theme: The Christian Hope

Dear God,
   I understand and believe in the Christian hope, grounded in Jesus' resurrection, that after our physical death, our life continues with you in another realm.
   I believe that 'he will wipe away every tear from their eyes, and death shall be no more, neither shall there be mourning nor crying nor pain any more.' I believe this in my heart. But what I don't find easy to understand God is that Christ died for me and in so doing my sins and the sins of the world have been forgiven and atoned for. Can it really be that simple? I know it in my head, but only now and then do I get glimpses of understanding in my heart.

Everyone around me seems to understand it perfectly, but do they God? Or do they feel like me that they ought to? Anyway, would such an horrific, earth shattering saving event be all that easy to comprehend, or does our perception and understanding deepen and widen the further we go on the Christian journey?

Would St Jude's be shattered or relieved that their rector's wife sometimes only sees through a glass very darkly?

Audrey

Tuesday 10th October
Paulinus, Bishop, Missionary, 644

Dear God,
Samuel Smudge is thirteen today. He got a tube of Good Dog Choc Drops and a new squeaky toy in the shape of a marrow bone.

He started his day by lifting his leg against the pram of Madge Dunbar's grandchild, and ended it by digging up an old bone together with Tom's Spider lilies.

Oh God, when he dies could it be on his beloved bean-bag? Is it wrong to love a dog so much? I don't trust people who don't like dogs or music.

Audrey

PS   There are only sixty-one shopping days to Christmas.

Saturday 14th October

Dear God,
Anthony appeared at the rectory at 9.30am, left his washing and took away my toasted sandwich-maker. Says he'll be

back tomorrow night to collect his ironing. He's only been gone a week or so, but it was so good to see him. I wish Derek were nearer.

Audrey

Sunday 15th October
Twenty-second Sunday after Pentecost
Theme: The Two Ways

Dear God,

Today's theme is 'The Two Ways', but the only way we can come to you is through Jesus Christ.

The collect for today began with, 'Stir up, O Lord, the wills of your faithful people.' Now this should have concentrated my mind on the stirring up of our wills to new efforts in our spiritual life as we approach the start of the new Christian year on Advent Sunday.

Instead my mind flew to a mid year resolution I'd made in June that this Christmas the family would eat a Christmas pud from Marks and Spencer, like it and not know its origin. The connection being that today used to be 'stir up' Sunday when it was customary for all the members of a family to take it in turns to stir the newly prepared Christmas pudding.

Luckily Mother's away at friends for the weekend otherwise we'd all be stirring away this afternoon and Christmas fever would have begun. This year I'm confining all preparations to December only. I won't let them hijack September, October and November as well.

Audrey

Wednesday 18th October
St Luke the Evangelist

Dear God,

Woke up this morning and thought I'd passed away and gone to heaven. Martin was at my side with a cup of tea and the newspaper. 'How nice,' I purred.

'What d'you want?' asked Tom surfacing next to me.

'He's just being kind,' I said.

'Twenty pounds will do,' said Martin, 'I'll pay you back as soon as I get a Saturday job.'

Moral: there's no such thing as a free cup of tea. Martin's rather cagey about what he wants it for. Tom says there's sure to be a girl behind it.

Audrey

Saturday 21st October

Dear God,

By 10 o'clock this morning Anthony had brought his washing, drunk two mugs of Nescafé, eaten half a packet of chocolate digestives and taken away my tennis racquet. I'm sure I remember a laundry room on the ground floor of his residence.

Audrey

Sunday 22nd October
Last Sunday after Pentecost
Theme: Citizens of Heaven

Dear God,
  How is it possible to know you? I may know about you, but do I *know* you? What does that small word 'know' mean?
  The Old Testament reading today was from Jeremiah, 'You will seek me and find me; when you seek me with all your heart, I will be found by you, says the Lord.' Does the answer lie in knowing you God with our heart, through your word, through the sacraments and within the body of the church, which for me is St Jude's, warts and all?
  St Paul says in his letter to the Philippians, 'But whatever gain I had, I counted as loss for the sake of Christ. Indeed I count everything as loss because of the surpassing worth of knowing Christ Jesus my Lord.' And in St John's Gospel we read, 'And this is eternal life, that they know thee the only true God, and Jesus Christ whom thou hast sent.'
  To know you God demands that I make space and time in my life. This takes commitment. There is no short cut, and it is so hard.

Audrey

Tuesday 24th October

Dear God,
  I just don't believe the conversation I had with Mother today.

  (Mother entering kitchen on way back from shopping.)
  Mother: Met that Mrs Bentworth-Smith in the High
           Street. Said she'd only just heard that Tom had
           been 'called'. 'Called'–I ask you! I said, 'Mrs

	Smith, only Baptists are called.' I leave out the Bentworth because it's pure affectation you know.
Me:	So how did you explain Tom's new vocation?
Mother:	I told her that having got to the top of the ladder in business...

(Enter Martin)

Martin:	He didn't like the view?
Mother:	...he wanted to take things easier and had decided himself to go into the church. Can't have her thinking he's not in control of his own life–'called' indeed!
Me:	Well Mother, he was 'called' you know. You don't decide to become a priest like you decide to take up cake decorating or aerobics.
Mother:	Well you didn't seem to hear the call.
Me:	Because I was and still am too attached to money and fillet of steak.
Mother:	Not to worry I've bought you two pounds of the best.
Martin:	Hooray! Red meat again.
Mother:	Well I can't bear to think of you suffering.
Me:	Oh Mother, we're not suffering.
Martin:	I am Nana. Look, (bareing gums), my gums are seriously white.
Mother:	Well I'd suffer living with that orange and purple patterned carpet in the hall and up the stairs, and those red and pink curtains in the study. Seems the last rector's wife went bananas, poor thing.

Audrey

Saturday 28th October
St Simon and St Jude, Apostles

Dear God,

Anthony dropped his washing off at 9.35am and was gone by 10am, armed with Tom's squash and badminton racquets.

I know that I haven't played tennis for years and that squash is not on Tom's agenda, but it's nice to have just one or two items around that testify to an active and well spent youth.

Asked Anthony if he'd discovered the laundromat in the college basement yet?

Today is the feast day of our own saint, St Jude. He shares it with another apostle, St Simon. From what I've been reading he enjoys great popularity as a powerful intercessor for those in desperate straits – that's me God. We'll be celebrating his feast day tomorrow.

Audrey

Sunday 29th October
Ninth Sunday before Christmas
Theme: the Creation

Dear God,

Started with the processional hymn 'Christ is made the sure foundation' this morning in honour of St Jude. Later the choir sang a special anthem to mark the occasion, Tarquin Barber doing the solo part.

Our Sunday school is awash with the Barber family progeny. They're all either sisters, brothers or cousins to each other, with a nine year old uncle and a ten year old aunt thrown in. Tarquin's brother Damian, aged four and a half years with red hair and built like a little tank, joined the Sunday school today.

During the offertory hymn the Sunday school came over

from the hall, tip toeing down the side aisles to the first three pews.

Today was Damian's first visit to 'God's house' and, climbing up onto the front pew, with his hands on his hips and his bright blue eyes sweeping over the congregation, the choir and the servers, and lingering fleetingly on Tom, said in a loud voice, 'So where's God?'

Today's report from Sunday school was written and read out by Jenna and Emma before the final blessing.

Jenna: First of all we sang 'Jesus wants me for a sunbeam.'

Emma: And then Brenda told us how Joseph's brothers were nasty to him and threw him into a big hole.

Jenna: And then we sang, 'When I needed a neighbour were you there, were you there?'

Emma: And then we prayed for all the hungry people in the world.

Jenna: And then we made chocolate brownies in the kitchen and ate them all up.

Emma: And then we drew pictures of Joseph's brothers throwing him into the hole.

Brenda: And here they are.

At which point three pews stood up turned around and held up their pictures.

'Schools should teach them more about perspective and less about sex,' growled Major Crabtree next to me.

Audrey

Tuesday 31st October
Saints and Martyrs of the Reformation Era

Dear God,

Took Sam to the vet because he can't walk far without panting. The vet said his heart's not at all good. It didn't stop him from getting a good nip at a champagne coloured poodle wearing a red knitted jacket on the way in though, and a few scratches from a terrified moggie on the way out.

He loves his pills–thinks they're more Good Dog Choc Drops.

Audrey

Wednesday 1st November
All Saints Day

Dear God,

I've lost. The build up to Christmas has already begun and it's only the 1st of November. Mother rang this morning to say she'd buy the turkey–hooray–and would I please remember when I'm making the Christmas cake, the pies and the mincemeat, which she expects I'll be making soon, that she doesn't eat candied peel. I haven't even thought about them yet, except the pud of course.

Martin's Christmas present list has appeared on the kitchen notice board already, between the family's dental appointments and Delia's Curried Nut Roast recipe. He keeps bringing it up to date, but as of the 1st of November it reads:

Martin's Xmas List

1. Porshe (ha ha - only joking!)
2. Golf clubs (not joking) - even second hand ones will do and I don't mind if it's a combined from Mum Dad + Nana.
3. Freddy Mercury's tape 'Tie your mother Down' - leave Derek to get this, you won't like the words Mum.
4. Musical Socks - those that play Jingle Bells - promise not to wear them to church.
5. After shave pong - Brut will do or even Denim Stud.
6. Jumbo Tin of chocs + toffees (If you can't manage quantity + quality I'll settle for quantity.
PS Remember God loves a cheerful giver!
PPS Remember also not to penalise me because my birthday's three days before Xmas - no joint presents please! I'll publish my birthday list tomorrow which will be more serious!!

Oh God, it seems only yesterday he was writing to Father Christmas asking for everything in Hamley's and ending with, 'Have a nice ride'.

Audrey

Thursday 2nd November
All Souls Day. Commemoration of the faithful departed

Dear God,
   Just been watching a TV programme *Forty Plus*. Claire Rayner says if you don't know who you are by the time you're forty you never will.
   Sent for make-up sheet for 'Forty Plus' faces.

Audrey

Saturday 4th November

Dear God,

If the induction on the 30th August didn't launch Tom into the parish, tonight certainly did. He'd been asked to open the parish's annual fireworks display. All that was required of him was to strike a match. Instead he made a unilateral decision that the occasion should start with a bang. He packed an empty tin can with fireworks, buried it in the ground and, after telling the crowd to stand well back he lit the fuse. Well God, it must have rivalled the bang at the start of creation.

A cheer went up and a broad grin spread over Tom's face. He looked like a naughty but satisfied ten year old as he and his dog collar disappeared in a cloud of smoke.

'Wonder if his sermons are as powerful?' said a voice behind me.

'Probably the first time he's set anything on fire,' mused another.

Anthony didn't appear with his washing this morning. Rang later to say that Tina was doing it with hers. He's taken the hint and I'm consumed with guilt. I've rejected my son and his washing. So what's another few years of shirts, socks and jeans until he finds himself a permanent cook, house-keeper, nurse, laundry maid, picker up of clothes and dolly bird.

Tom said, 'And it's about time too.' He's quite hard you know God for a Clerk in Holy Orders.

Who's Tina?

Audrey

Sunday 5th November
Eighth Sunday before Christmas
Theme: The Fall

Dear God,

Helped with the Sunday school this morning as Brenda had flu. The task was made easier by the absence of both Rosey and Stephen Barber with chicken pox.

Using today's theme of the Fall, they learnt how the serpent had tempted Eve to eat the fruit from the forbidden tree and how the Lord God had driven Adam and Eve out of the Garden of Eden because of their disobedience.

I learnt that the wife of Lauren's Uncle Jim had left him because of the four foot long snake he keeps under their bed, and how Jason's grandfather, who'd been bitten by a puff adder in Africa, had gouged out his flesh with his penknife, sucked out the poison and spat it out.

We discussed what we thought the Garden of Eden had looked like, the end result being halfway between Jungle

Book and Disney Land, with you God sitting on a cloud or up a tree.

Before going over to join St Jude's congregation they made a frieze. Right in the middle, between the gorillas, flowers and monkey ropes, was a literal interpretation by Billy Barber of Adam and Eve in the back of a long stretch automobile being driven out of the Garden by you God at the wheel.

Audrey

Monday 6th November
Leonard, c 559

Dear God,

General Synod meets today. I lit a candle for them because they need all the help they can get. Tom says a rocket would have been better.

Audrey

Tuesday 7th November

Dear God,

Tom asked his class at St Jude's C of E School this morning to compose and write down a short prayer. One little boy wrote: 'Dear God life is a bit ruff sumtimes but thank you for berthdays and chrismus amen.'

His teacher confirmed that this was a fair reflection of his home life–mostly unhappy. How sad that one so young should have such an unhappy life that he poured it out in this way.

Tom told them that prayer was about talking to you God and telling you about their deepest thoughts and feelings; the good feelings, the sad feelings and those of which we are ashamed.

I'd like to think God that when things get 'ruff' for him, he'll always feel that he can talk to you.

Audrey

Saturday 11th November
Martin, Bishop of Tours, 397

Dear God,

Pity poor Tom and all clergy tomorrow. It's Remembrance Sunday and delivering a sermon is like straying into a minefield. Last year a visiting priest beat too many 'swords into ploughshares' and 'spears into pruning hooks' and was almost lynched by a mob of medal jangling majors, colonels and ex-Waafs from the vestry to the lych-gate.

No sign of Anthony and his washing again this morning. My guilt's lessened and I'm beginning to warm to this Tina. Has he really flown the nest God? Tom says he thinks not.

Audrey

Sunday 12th November
Seventh Sunday before Christmas
Remembrance Sunday
Theme: The Election of God's People: Abraham

Dear God,

It's all over. All three verses of 'The Queen' sung and two minutes silence kept, broken only by a thin whistle from someone's hearing aid.

Tom decided that, as he wouldn't be able to convince

them about 'ploughshares' and 'pruning hooks', he'd confuse them with Wilfred Owen's poem 'Dulce et Decorum est'.

Colonel Hawkridge deemed it a splendid sermon. Major Crabtree said, 'Well done Padré,' followed by Miss Flowers who said she'd been a land girl and had a lovely war.

Tom was quite chuffed and let Martin have a sherry before lunch.

Audrey

Monday 13th November
Charles Simeon, Pastor, Preacher, 1836.
Britius, Bishop

Dear God,
Tom woke this morning full of self-hate and loathing, denouncing himself as a coward and hypocrite over the 'ploughshare' and 'pruning hook' business, declaring that he was just a 'priest in their pocket', that for too long they'd had him on their own terms, that he wasn't living up to his ordination vows, that he should be unfrocked, that he wasn't a ruddy padré and that he'd sock it to them next year.

Audrey

Tuesday 14th November

Dear God,
Met Philippa Hart in Marks & Spencer today. Haven't seen her since Tom's ordination.

'What's it like going to bed with a priest?' she shouted across the knicker counter. She's never quite come down to earth since 'The Thorn Birds'.

I know she never sets foot in church God, but would you

reserve her one of your many mansions, (with room service of course), because she makes me laugh.

Audrey

Wednesday 15th November
Machutus, Bishop, c 564

Dear God,
Give me patience and restraint. If Madge Dunbar mentions the good works, the talents, the achievements and superb peach chutney and feather-like sponge cakes of my predecessor once more I'LL HIT HER!
Oh God, why haven't I got that 'locked-in' flavour? Why can't I forbear?

Audrey

Sunday 19th November
Sixth Sunday before Christmas
Theme: The Promise of Redemption: Moses

Dear God,
Between the 8 o'clock and the 10.30 services this morning a Mrs Lewis phoned. Why didn't Tom condemn Scientology from the pulpit? Why didn't the church spell out the Ten Commandments anymore? Why didn't they teach children the difference between right and wrong? The church was failing the nation, they were losing their grip, no wonder pews were empty.
After ascertaining that Mrs Lewis was not a parishioner of any church, but rather a great fan of the Sunday papers, just managing to maintain his grip, Tom invited her to join us at

St Jude's next Sunday. This had the desired effect. The conversation was terminated.

This evening there was a phone call from a Mrs Wellington who wanted to book St Jude's for her Fiona's wedding to Group Captain McWilliams next July. It transpired that she lived in a parish twenty miles away, had no connections with St Jude's at all, but thought when passing the other day, that it would make a wonderful setting for Fiona's wedding, especially the lych-gate – 'Lovely setting for the photographs, Rector.'

Ten minutes after Tom had told her it was not on, Fiona's irate father was on the phone threatening to report him to the bishop or, failing him, to the Archbishop. Tom said he must feel free to do so, but advised him rather to opt for his own parish church, even if it were between McDonald's and the gas tank.

Audrey

Wednesday 22nd November
Cecilia, Virgin and Martyr at Rome, 230

Dear God,

Went to Father Gary's induction in the adjoining parish at St Bede's tonight. The woman next to me whispered, 'That must be the new vicar's wife.'

'How do you know?' I asked.

''Cause she looks like a "clergy" wife,' she said.

What do clergy wives look like God?

Father Gary wears sky blue and mint green clerical shirts and has a moustache.

Audrey

PS   Mother says she sees trouble brewing at St Bede's.

Friday 24th November

Dear God,

There's a notice on Martin's bedroom door–'Love me Love my Room'. Now this is difficult because it's Armageddon in there. I'm allowed in once a week to clean and to retrieve all the missing coffee mugs.

Today it was worse than usual. The pile of clothes, books, plates, coffee mugs, windsurfing magazines and wet towels on his desk has reached critical proportions. On the wall above this impending avalanche is his current philosophy– 'A tidy desk is a sign of a tiny mind'.

Audrey

Sunday 26th November
Fifth Sunday before Christmas
Theme: The Remnant of Israel

Dear God,

The Old Testament reading from Exodus 20:2-17 began this morning with 'I am the Lord your God...' and I was back at the Dominican Convent where I was educated. While the Catholics had their catechism we non-Catholics had the Ten Commandments.

To break a commandment was a mortal sin and each one was taken apart, examined, expanded on and applied to our daily lives, except for the seventh commandment, 'Thou shalt not commit adultery'.

Over the years this commandment became an area of brilliant inexactitude and fudging. Each year a different nun would try to convey the dreadfulness of such a sin without telling us exactly what it was.

One year Sister Mary Agnes explained it as taking that which didn't belong to one, but this seemed to be what the eighth commandment was all about. The next year Sister Felicitas said that married people shouldn't look at other people which seemed a bit odd.

By the age of twelve we'd put two and two together. Now we waited eagerly for the seventh commandment to come up just to observe the confusion and embarrassment it caused.

I wonder if they're still learning the Ten Commandments at my Alma Mater today God. I hope so. I wonder too if they're also being told, 'Girls, always make sure you're wearing clean underwear and *never* hold it together with a safety pin. You never know when you're going to be run over.' Even now I'm nervous crossing the road wearing a safety pin.

Well God, Mr Venn should be pleased with today's reading and sermon. He links the rising crime rate directly to ignorance of the Ten Commandments.

Audrey

Thursday 30th November
St Andrew the Apostle

Dear God,
 The Diocesan surveyor arrived at 12 o'clock today to do his quinquennial inspection of the rectory. I don't know what he had on his list after his inspection, but the state of the kitchen floor was at the top of mine.
 Remembering what the bishop's wife had said I played the health and safety card. I managed to whip up a really disgusting picture for him of how everything that drops finds its way into the spaces between the shrinking floor tiles.
 I don't think it was the gravy, raw egg, mashed potato and squashed peas lodged between the tiles that swung it for me, but rather Sammy's occasional regurgitations which got me the royal assent for a new floor covering.
 Spent a lovely afternoon at the floor tile shops. It's so nice spending someone else's money.

Audrey

Saturday 2nd December
Nicholas Ferrar, Deacon,
Founder of Little Gidding Community, 1637

Dear God,
 Disaster struck our middle son last week. He had just pressed the digits at the cashpoint in the wall outside the bank, which he had done so many, many times before, when suddenly there flashed upon the screen those dreaded words, 'Your request exceeds your account balance. Amount available 22p'. Well, he was at the rectory before you could say 'bankruptcy', clutching a six pack of Foster's lager and a packet of cheese and onion chips.
 'What', he cried, 'are they on about?' He was a Mars Bar away from starvation and he knew it.

'Son you can't take out what you haven't put in,' I said gently, hating the cruel world. He didn't actually say 'Why not?', but I could have sworn I heard him thinking it.

To give him his due though God, he didn't give up easily. No, he tried that cash point again the next day and the next. Then, in what you could hardly call a blinding revelation, he realised there was a relationship between incomings and outgoings.

But, every cloud has a silver lining. He's kept the same girl friend now for two weeks because he can't afford to wine and dine a new one at the moment. His spots have cleared up too. The shops are feeling the pinch though as the Big Spender lies low.

But there's light at the end of the tunnel for him, the bank and the shops at the dawn of a new academic year in ten months time, and another round of grant cheques to set the whole economy ticking over once more.

Audrey

Sunday 3rd December
Advent Sunday
Theme: The Advent Hope

Dear God,

Today is the beginning of the season of Advent and the beginning of the ecclesiastical year. There will be no flowers in church until Christmas, no 'Gloria in Excelsis' will be sung or said at the Eucharist, and the liturgical colour will be purple, except on saints' days or feast days of martyrs, when it will be white or red.

The service started with the sentence, 'Now is the time to wake out of sleep: for now our salvation is nearer than when we first believed.' We sang that lovely Advent hymn that expresses deep longing for the coming of Christ, 'O come O come, Emmanuel'. We were told that Advent, like Lent, is also a time for reflection and self examination. It is a time for preparation for Christmas and for the second coming of Christ as judge on the last day, and that the church in her wisdom had set aside this time to enable us to do just that. But, though the colour purple is associated with despair, mourning and our own unworthiness, we are uplifted because Advent gives us that wonderful thought 'God comes'. It's for this that we prepare.

Our minds were taken to the end of Advent and to those words in the book of Isaiah:

> To us a child is born, to us a son is given; and the government will be upon his shoulder, and his name will be called 'Wonderful Counsellor, Mighty God, Everlasting Father, Prince of Peace'.

If our Advent has been used wisely they will have meaning and understanding such as we have not known before.

Today is also my birthday, which always prompts reflection in me. I'm not sure I improve with age God. I haven't murdered anyone or robbed a bank yet, but my pride, intolerance, resentments and petty jealousies are still alive and well. They won't make headlines, but they do relegate me to the category so aptly described in the Book of Common Prayer as a 'miserable offender'.

But my family still loves and tolerates me, warts and all. Anthony popped over. Derek phoned to say a parcel was on its way and Tom gave me the handbag I'd been eyeing in Army & Navy. Martin came up with Thornton's chocolates and Mother laid on a big roast dinner–'to have a break from mince', as she put it.

Audrey

Wednesday 6th December
Nicholas, Bishop of Myra, c 326

Dear God,

It all became clear to me in the New Testament reading at Communion this morning. I'm a Mary and the rest of St Jude's are Marthas. Even their looks say, 'Don't just sit there, do something!'

Madge Dunbar says she can't just sit and do nothing and Doris Stubbs says she'd never buy an automatic car because she wouldn't know what to do with her hands. She could scratch her head God. I blame it all on the Protestant work ethic.

Tom is trying to promote a more contemplative spirit in St Jude's services. He's been encouraging private prayer and meditation by introducing silences into the services, his strategy being, 'Softly, softly, catcha da monkey'. Some are very unnerved by this and start gathering their things together, others fall asleep.

But God, even this Mary finds it very difficult to quieten her racing mind and do what the psalmist says: 'Be still, and know that I am God'. I too need help to enter into that silence and stillness of which you are the centre.

Audrey

Thursday 7th December
Ambrose, Bishop of Milan, Teacher of the Faith, 397

Dear God,

Received my 'Forty Plus' make-up fact sheet this morning. I need about twelve items before I can show my face in public again. But the most important of all has to be the concealer; a sort of facial Polyfilla without which one should not even consider bringing the milk in from the porch.

Of course God, if you'd sent me a daughter instead of three sons I'd have known all this.

Audrey

Friday 8th December
Conception of B.V. Mary

Dear God,
Made another sortie into Armageddon this morning as we're low on coffee mugs again. Well, something's happened. Martin's desk has been swept bare (mainly onto the floor) of all books, clothes, plates and crisp packets etc., and there in the middle in splendid isolation is a photograph of someone who's signed herself 'Cuddles'.

This must be serious to clear such a large area. Who is Cuddles? Well, if I can't find out, his brothers will. I'm beginning to like her already if that's the effect she has.

Audrey

Sunday 10th December
Second Sunday in Advent
Theme: The Word of God in the Old Testament

Dear God,
Today is Bible Sunday and the collect for the day is that splendid one composed by Cranmer in the Book of Common Prayer.

Blessed Lord, who hast caused all holy Scriptures to be written for our learning: Grant that we may in such wise hear them, read, mark, learn, and inwardly digest them, that by patience and comfort of thy holy Word, we may embrace and ever hold fast the blessed hope of everlasting life, which thou hast given us in our Saviour Jesus Christ.

It's sad that many churches omit the Old Testament from their worship and miss so much of your revelation of yourself. As Tom pointed out in his sermon today, 'Starting to read the Bible at St Mathew's Gospel, as if nothing happened before then, is like coming into a theatre on the third act of a three act play–it just doesn't make much sense. We can only hope to understand the Gospels against the background of the history of the Jewish people.'

I sometimes think God that the Old Testament is nearer our world today than the New Testament, because the majority of people still live as if Jesus had not yet come.

It's encouraging to me that you used people who were frail and fallible like most of us and, even though their understanding was limited, you accepted them and worked through them in the world.

Mrs Venn told me yesterday that she'd volunteered to help Harry, our alcoholic illiterate gardener, with his reading and writing. She's thrilled.

Harry told me about it this morning, smiling from ear to ear. I don't know which one you're working through God, but it's brought new purpose into both their lives.

Audrey

Tuesday 12th December

Dear God,
    Just eaten Christmas dinner number one with the Men's Society at the Spotted Cow.

Audrey

Wednesday 13th December
Ember Day, Lucy, Virgin and Martyr

Dear God,
   Just eaten Christmas dinner number two with the Mothers' Union at the Dog and Duck, where Mrs Tonkins crossed walking sticks with Mrs Mason.
   Tom muttered something about the Christmas spirit, which it was of course.

Audrey

Thursday 14th December
John of the Cross, Mystic, Teacher of the Faith, 1591

Dear God,
   Just eaten Christmas dinner number three at our Church of England Infants' School, doubled up on six inch high chairs with our chests on our knees and our chins on the tables, and not much room for the figgy pudding.
   Spent the afternoon helping to prepare the oranges for our Junior School's Christingle service in St Jude's tomorrow afternoon, a service introduced to the Anglican Church by the Children's Society in 1968.
   The symbolism of an orange girded with a red ribbon, pierced by four cocktail sticks bearing raisins and sweets and a candle stuck in the top will become clear tomorrow. It will be my first Christingle service.

Audrey

Friday 15th December
Ember Day

Dear God,

This afternoon St Jude's came alive with children and parents for Christingle. For some parents this would be their only encounter with the church this Christmas.

As the children processed around the church, each holding a spiked orange with a lighted candle on top, we sang 'Once in royal David's city'.

Tom then elicited from the children what the orange, the cocktail sticks, the sweetmeats, the red ribbon and the candle on top represented. For many it was their 2nd, 3rd, or 4th Christingle and so they were able to volunteer that:

a) The orange itself represents the world which God has created for all of us to live in and that we must always work to see that there is no one who is hungry, cold, lonely or unloved.

b) The four cocktail sticks represent spring, summer, autumn and winter, the four seasons of the year which God has created.

c) The raisins and sweets impaled on the sticks are the fruits of the earth–crops, clean water, grass, trees and all that grows.

d) The red ribbon around the orange is the blood which Jesus shed for us on Good Friday when he was crucified so that our sins might be forgiven and that we might have eternal life.

e) The candle on the top is the light of Jesus who is the Light of the World; who shines in our lives and who shines out of each one of us when we listen to him and do his will.

They were told that theirs are the hands that God uses to heal the sick; theirs are the hearts who forgive and love their neighbours and so bring peace; and theirs are the eyes and ears that see and hear when people need help.

Classes one and two then sang the carol 'The Friendly Beasts'. There followed a playlet, *The First Christingle*, by John, Cheryl, Anita and Jessica, during which most of the little ones in front ate up the fruits of the earth.

After the Christingle hymn came the presentation of the purses, money collected by each class for the Children's Society. Then classes 3, 4 and 5 sang 'Silent night, holy night'. James read from Isaiah and Elizabeth from Matthew. By now the four seasons had disappeared from the world.

During the prayers offered by Robert and Michelle from class 5, the red ribbons began to slip. I watched as tilted candles dripped wax onto pews and orange juice escaped from the world squeezed by little hot hands and I thought of the Holy Dusters.

Before 'Away in a manger' the candles were snuffed out. During the second verse there was panic in the third row. A budding pyromaniac had hidden his light beneath a bushel, as it were, and now the guttering flame had spread to the paper collar at the base of his candle and to his hymn sheet.

Yes, the Holy Dusters will suck their breath in tomorrow as they unstick the pews. Yes, it was chaotic at times, but when I heard a small boy explaining again to his mother afterwards what the orange, cocktail sticks, sweetmeats, ribbon and lighted candle represented, I knew it had all been worthwhile.

Audrey

Saturday 16th December
Ember Day

Dear God,

I'd actually got it together this morning. By 10.30am the dishes were washed, Derek and Anthony's rooms made up because they'll be home for Christmas this afternoon, my facial Polyfilla on and the dog walked. All was well with the world.

Then Martin rose from the dead and asked if he could have a 'rave up' at the rectory on his birthday next week. Fear clutched my stomach. I felt sick. Visions of Sodom and Gomorrah floated past my eyes—drink, drugs, sex, vandalism and mindless music at 110 decibels. After a deep breath and an arrow prayer for calm I played for time, 'I'll discuss it with your father,' I said.

Again I could see the headlines in *The Church Times, The Tablet*, the local paper and the parish magazine—'Ravings at the Rectory' with the subtitle 'St Jude's Rectory—Den of Iniquity'.

'So what does a "rave up" entail?' I asked casually.

'Nothing much Mum—just birds, booze and a few nibbles.'

Nibbles of what, crisps, cheese straws, sausages on sticks or necks and ears!? Mother's right. It's the schools that are to blame.

God, I can't talk to Tom about it tonight because he's

finishing his sermon and preparing for the Chapter meeting next Tuesday on The Church and Homosexuality.

Maybe they should be discussing 'The Church–teenage "rave ups", especially in rectories.' Oh God, surely 'rave up' and rectory are a contradiction in terms? If they're not, they should be.

Anthony and Derek never had a 'rave up', they just had a few friends and 'rave ups' happened at other people's houses, so why does Martin have to be different? Anyway, I was planning to have a family meal at The Stag which I thought macho enough.

Why did I have Martin at such a hectic time of the year God? Well, one doesn't think, does one?

What were Tom and I going to do while the hordes took over? 'Just make yourself scarce, that's all,' said Martin.

Well I wasn't going to be any more scarce than upstairs in bed with a quarter pound of chocolates and a Barbara Cartland.

Audrey

Sunday 17th December
Third Sunday in Advent
Theme: The Forerunner

Dear God,

Why don't I take things in my stride like Tom does? When the 'rave up' came up at lunch today he simply turned to Martin and said, 'No alcohol, no drugs, no vandalism, no bodies lying around in dark places upstairs, downstairs, in cupboards or in the garden; no food or drink on the furniture, carpets, walls or ceilings, no eardrum shattering music and we're not going out. Right? I'll be in my study and your mother will be in bed with Barbara Cartland and a quarter pound of chocolates. Right?' Oh God, am I so boringly predictable?

I almost felt sorry for Martin, not much of a 'rave up'; but he seemed quite happy and after lunch was on the phone to his friend Dale.

'I would never have thought of mentioning the bit about the ceiling,' I said to Tom later in bed.

'Well you've never been a seventeen-year-old male. I have,' he replied.

Audrey

Tuesday 19th December

Dear God,

In my house there aren't enough mansions. The Sunday school teachers are in the sitting-room cutting out the Wise Men's crowns. The mothers are in the kitchen glueing and glittering angels' wings for the Nativity play tomorrow. In the dining-room the Men's Society are making final preparations for their Christmas outing to *Babes in the Wood*. Tom and the churchwardens are locked in the study agonising on how to get more 'bums on seats'. The boys have fled to their bedrooms to don their 'trannies' and I'm in bed at eight with my book.

Audrey

Wednesday 20th December
Ember Day

Dear God,

Wise Men's crowns, glittering angels' wings, stripey drying up cloths, bath towels, bedspreads, curtains, a ton of tinsel and loads of safety pins all came together this evening at 7.30pm in the church hall.

Yes, there were too many angels. Yes, I know there's no mention in the Bible of cattle and sheep being present at Jesus' birth in the stable. I know the star shouldn't have moved from north to south, and yes, I know that whoever chose Mary needs their head read, but the parents loved it.

I've lost my voice God. It finally cracked tonight between 'bring me ale' and 'bring me wine'. I never want to hear another carol.

Audrey

Thursday 21st December
St Thomas the Apostle

Dear God,
The undertaker came round with a bottle of whisky and a bottle of Bailey's Irish for Tom. Jolly nice of him. It's not as if he has to drum up business!

Audrey

Friday 22nd December
Ember Day

Dear God,
Martin was born at 2.30am seventeen years ago today. He arrived along with the Christmas cards, turkey, nuts and raisins, and wrapping paper. He entered the world in a hurry and the doctor who delivered him said from the other end of the table, 'Boys are really very nice Audrey.' That's how I knew I was now the mother of three sons.

Just before he left for college this morning Cuddles phoned to wish him happy birthday. 'You'll see her tonight Mum,' he said when I asked what she was like. Well I wouldn't if I were in bed with a quarter pound of chocolates and my book, would I?

Derek and Anthony have refused to be involved in the 'rave up' in any way, something about having 'put away childish things.'

Dale, with green hair and perforated earlobes, arrived early with his box of tapes. Then about 8.30pm the hordes started to arrive and I found I could have a good view of them from the small front bedroom.

I've decided that the girl wearing the shocking pink fluorescent pants and black T shirt with the words 'Hi Good Looking' has to be Cuddles. I'd prefer the one with the ponytail and the T shirt bearing the words 'Save the Earth'.

9.20pm. Nothing much seems to be going on downstairs. It's all so quiet God. What *can* they be doing?

9.25pm. The earth's just moved, the chocs have fallen off the bed, the cat's dived into the wardrobe and the rectory windows are about to fall out of their Grade II listed frames. Someone's flicked the switch on 'Tie your mother down'. It's just a matter of time before Miss Willis rings and the police appear on the doorstep.

10.05pm. All quiet again.

11.00pm. Still quiet. Oh God, far *too* quiet. What are they doing now? INJECTING THEMSELVES!?

11.30pm. Tom has just come up to bed. Says they're all sitting around Dale who's entertaining them with conjuring tricks. I'm so ashamed God of all the unworthy thoughts scurrying around in my mind.

11.45pm. Oh God, they're all tying their mother down again, the cat's gone back into the wardrobe and I CAN'T SLEEP!

Audrey

Saturday 23rd December
Ember Day

Dear God,

Someone's stolen baby Jesus and it's the Crib service tomorrow. If it helps he's twice the size of Mary, who's twice the size of Joseph, who's three times the size of the cow. Last seen he was wearing a Peaudouce fully elasticated nappy and a Garfield T shirt.

You know God, I was wrong. Cuddles was the one with the pony tail and into saving the earth.

Audrey

Sunday 24th December
Fourth Sunday in Advent (Christmas Eve)
Theme: The Annunciation

Dear God,

We've found baby Jesus. Alison Louise took him home for the night because she couldn't sleep without him.

At the half hour Crib service this afternoon St Jude's turned into a snake pit. Tiny tots writhed under and over the pews and staggered and crawled up and down the aisle waving plastic bottles and hymn books. I think we should hold the next one at Mothercare!

Audrey

Later.

Dear God,

The shops are shut and the roads almost deserted. Had to make a last dash to Tesco when Mother said, 'Of course you've got the cranberry sauce,' and also because the boys persuaded me that Christmas began last night and have already devoured most of the mixed nuts.

Mother moved into the rectory this morning for the festive season with the turkey, her electric blanket, a hot water bottle, two large suitcases and a bottle of port.

For a while the turkey became the focal point as the family gathered to view it on the kitchen table. The butcher's promised Mother that it's been hanging for at least two weeks. It must be one of those I have avoided looking at. Mother prodded its plump thighs with her very experienced index finger and said that at £1.40 a pound you could have bought the whole farmyard in her day.

Tom, taking a break from his Christmas sermon preparation, prodded it with his very inexperienced finger saying, 'He's a beaut.' How can he God, a man of the cloth?

Derek's christened the turkey Fred. It's all so obscene. I wish he'd turn into a nut cutlet.

Martin says he's planning to become a vegetarian after Christmas dinner. Derek reminded him he'd said the same last year.

It's 11.00pm, the last present's been wrapped and placed under the tree. It's almost time to go over to St Jude's for the midnight service, the first Communion of Christmas and our first at St Jude's.

Audrey

Monday 25th December
Christmas Day

Dear God,

It's 1.30am, it's −5° outside and we've just come back from the midnight service. It's Christmas Day. Advent is over and the liturgical colour is white.

The service ended with the words 'The Glory of the Lord shall be revealed, and all mankind shall see it'. And in some small way that glory was reflected in St Jude's tonight in the ivory, cream and gold of the flowers, the gleaming brass work, the altar frontal, the beautiful St Jude's cope that Tom wore and the lighted candles set in circles of holly and red ribbon at the end of each pew.

'They've come out of the woodwork,' we whispered to each other as we moved closer together in the pews to make room while chairs were brought over from the hall, books shared and extra wine and communion wafers set out.

Doris Stubbs had her brother with her from Solihull.

Madge Dunbar had her son and daughter-in-law and three grandchildren down from Scotland. There were Mr and Mrs Williams from the newsagents, Rodriguez from the amusement arcade and the butcher who'd hung Fred on a hook for two weeks.

Already Father Benson and Father Geoffrey were robing in the vestry ready to concelebrate with Tom. There was excitement in the air – a magic.

At 11.30pm with the opening bars of 'Once in royal David's city' the choir vestry doors opened and out came the procession led by the crucifer. When it reached the back of the church the crib was blessed then it moved on up the centre aisle between the avenue of lighted candles.

We heard again how nearly 2000 years ago you revealed yourself to the world; how you came in your Son to live and love and die here on earth with us. Gone now was the old idea that you are a jealous God who punishes at some capricious whim. Here was a God of love in whose eyes greatness isn't to be found in position or power, wealth or cleverness but in humility, in serving others and being child-like in faith.

We were reminded that at the first Christmas something incredible and wonderful happened:

> And the Word became flesh and dwelt among us, full of grace and truth.

The Prince of Peace had come among us.

Audrey

Christmas Night

Dear God,
  It's been a funny day, so much that is spiritual jostling with so much that's material and excessive.

By 12.30pm Tom was back from St Jude's and finished for the day. An hour later Fred was on the table surrounded by seven of us including Miss Flowers who would otherwise have been on her own. Sammy had positioned himself under the table for anything that dropped and Pooky the cat was in the kitchen licking out the pots.

Karen phoned Anthony to declare her undying love, which lasted until the second helping of the turkey. Then he declared his undying love, which lasted till the flaming Christmas pud passed him in the hall.

The boys insisted they make the Christmas punch; the ingredients being the same as last year except, that is, for a mystery bottle of something which caused much hilarity and rolling of the eyes. Expressions like, 'far out man,' 'off the planet,' and 'wicked' flew around as the three of them bent over the steaming bowl like the witches from Macbeth. Obviously it needed a government health warning and was definitely a case of the whole being more explosive than the sum of the parts.

By the time the Queen's speech had started Miss Flowers was nodding off. She surfaced again when the presents were opened whispering to me that I must be very proud of my three sons. Well of course I'm proud God. I'm proud I've survived them and I'm proud that so far they haven't killed each other!

Martin gave Derek a small plastic tub on which it said, 'Grow your own Porsche,' and a similar one to Tom which said, 'Grow your own French maid.' There was a hurried switch. He'd got them mixed up thank goodness! They were filled with vermiculite and had to be kept in the warmth.

Derek gave Tom a pair of Tom and Jerry underpants and Philippa had sent me some knickers which caused Miss Flowers to choke on her after dinner mint. Mother gave me a nightdress (much needed), Tom, Mother and I came up with the golf clubs for Martin, and Derek came up with the musical socks and Anthony the jumbo tin of chocs and toffees. Anthony gave Derek an apron with 'King of the

House,' and Martin and Derek gave Anthony a T shirt reading 'Go for it Loverboy'.

There were chocolates and notepaper for Miss Flowers, gloves, a Filofax and perfume for me from Tom, a bottle of port, slippers and a scarf for Mother, chews for Sammy and a ping pong ball for the cat.

At 4.30pm we all went for the traditional after Christmas dinner walk. First we met Doris Stubbs and her brother who she introduced as a pillar of his church in Solihull—treasurer, lay reader, chairman of the fund raising committee and the vicar's right hand man.

Further on we met Mrs Burt exercising her three dachshunds. She asked Tom if she could have his letter for the January magazine a week early as she was going away.

When in the distance we saw the Barber family approaching, we took a short cut back to the rectory and locked and bolted the doors.

By 5.30pm the family was baying for food again, so out came the mince pies and Christmas cake. After consuming a large slice, Mother said I should remind her to ferret out her mother's recipe which was always reliable.

The remains of the punch were reheated and consumed mainly by Anthony and the dregs by Sammy. Then they both disappeared from the scene; Anthony to moan quietly in his bed, Sammy to snore loudly in his basket.

That was Christmas God.

Audrey

PS   Who's Karen? Martin says she wears a nose stud!

Tuesday 26th December
Boxing Day
St Stephen the First Martyr

Dear God,
 On this the first day of Christmas, from his darkened bedroom Anthony said he'd kill Martin for sabotaging his love life. Martin had told Karen when she phoned at 7.30 this morning that Anthony had been as sick as a parrot all night and that he and Sammy were still literally 'punch drunk'.
 Of course God we should have stopped at 2.4 children. It's that extra 0.6 which is the catalyst and causes all the murder and mayhem in our house.

Audrey

Wednesday 27th December
St John the Evangelist

Dear God,
 On the second day of Christmas two heaps of iron rattled up the drive and parked outside the rectory. Each was held together with a large luminous sticker, the first reading, 'Windsurfers do it standing up', and the second, 'Aussies do it upside down'. It was Dale of the green hair, perforated earlobes and conjuring tricks and Steven, boyfriend of the 'Hi Goodlooking' T shirt.
 As Mother and Miss Willis were due back from their walk any minute another conjuring trick was urgently needed. Tom had a quick word in Martin's ear, who had an even quicker word in Dale's and Steven's ears and, hey presto, the stickers were now facing into the rhododendron bushes.
 I learnt later that the quick word in Martin's ear was, 'You have exactly thirty seconds my boy to get those stickers out

of sight or I'll stop your allowance'. His parenting skills aren't very kosher God, but they work!

Audrey

Thursday 28th December
The Holy Innocents

Dear God,

On the third day of Christmas I took all the things back to Marks & Spencer that didn't fit—the gloves that were too small, the nightdress that was too big, plus the knickers from Philippa I couldn't hang on the line.

Tom says he's keeping his Tom and Jerry underpants, so I'll just have to remember to hang them to dry under a sheet. The Porsche and the French maid are in the airing cupboard trying to germinate.

Audrey

Friday 29th December
Thomas Becket, Archbishop of Canterbury, 1170

Dear God,

On the fourth day of Christmas I received a nasty shock. I'd just been looking around at my three sons at dinner thinking I'd done quite a good job really; probably not damaged their psyches too much, none of them had twitches and they were all eating with their mouths shut, when Anthony blurted it all out.

He'd been absolutely terrified of *The Cat in the Hat* which I used to read to them when they were small before they went to bed. I know he was frightened of going upstairs in the dark God, but *The Cat in the Hat*!

What does this mean God? Well it means just how wrong one can be, but I was so tired of Noddy and Big Ears that Dr Seus's *The Cat in the Hat* came as a great humorous breath of fresh air. Then, blinded by my own enthusiasm, I'd followed it with *The Cat in the Hat Comes Back*–poor child! Martin and Derek now dredged up their terrors.

Martin had been terrified of the wooden spoon I waved around when they all got too much for me. Derek had been terrified of the look I gave them when they misbehaved in company which said, 'Just wait until we get home my boy. I'm going to hang you from the rafters and you won't be able to sit down for a week.'

Heaven knows what damage I've done and what memories I've etched on their minds. Maybe this accounts for Anthony falling for a girl with a nose stud, Martin's inability to shut the fridge door or put the lid back on the syrup tin, and Derek's serious nest building.

Audrey

Saturday 30th December
Josephine Butler, Social Reformer, Wife, Mother, 1906

Dear God,
  On the fifth day of Christmas none of the brothers Karamazov rose before 12 o'clock and when they did they occupied the phone for the rest of the day.

After breakfast Mrs O'Reilly phoned, 'Can the rector come round as soon as he can because my Paddy says there's voices coming out of the wallpaper?'

'Anyone seen my bones and hen's foot?' asked Tom.

Miss Willis says that Mrs O'Reilly calls up the rectory at least twice a year to deal with Paddy's voices. Tom says now he's seen the wallpaper he understands why!

Audrey

Sunday 31st December
Sunday after Christmas Day
Theme: The Presentation

Dear God,
  On the sixth day of Christmas Tom preached on 'Peace and Goodwill'. 'The peace that the baby lying in the manger was to preach about,' he said, 'was not about the external kind between nations, which is at best precarious, but the peace in the hearts of each one of us.

  'Jesus said, "If any man would come after me, let him deny himself and take up his cross daily and follow me". This dying to self and self-interest is the only route to everlasting peace in families and between neighbours and nations.'

  Peace and goodwill appears on many of our Christmas cards and immediately brings to mind wars, refugees, famine and Northern Ireland. Maybe God, more cards should read, 'May the peace of God which passes all understanding be in your hearts and minds this Christmas', for here is where true peace begins.

Audrey

Monday 1st January
The Naming of Jesus (or Circumcision of Christ)

Dear God,
  Happy New Year. Just come back from the traditional gathering at the lych-gate of St Jude's at midnight on the 31st of December.
  We arrived as the muffled bells were tolling out the last night of the old year. We thanked you God for the old year, for all the benefits we'd received and we asked your forgiveness where we had fallen short.

I always feel sad as the old year dies away, embodying as it does unfulfilled hopes, the passing of friends and loved ones, and change.

Upon the first stroke of twelve St Jude's bells, now unmuffled, rang out loud and clear in the sharp air joyously welcoming in the new year. They spread their hope over the parish: over the library, the corner shop, the post office, the duck pond, the Dog and Duck, over Michael from the choir, the Barber family and the Misses Patterson, warm beneath their crocheted bedspreads, and over Polly Nightingale who'd just prayed for the whole world.

We then prayed for your strength to go forward into the new year in hope and love. God, it is this hope, this 'triumph of hope over experience' that makes me saddest of all.

We ended with the first and last verse of a hymn which says it all:

> Through all the changing scenes of life,
> In trouble and in joy,
> The praises of my God shall still
> My heart and tongue employ.
>
> To Father, Son and Holy Ghost,
> The God whom we adore,
> Be glory, as it was, is now,
> And shall be evermore. Amen.

Audrey

Monday 1st January
Later

Dear God,
    This morning, on the seventh day of Christmas my family started to regroup. Having eaten the last of the mince pies,

the Christmas cake and the mixed nuts for breakfast, they homed in on their provider.

'And what New Year resolutions have you made?' asked Tom. 'To pursue a hobby I hope?'

'It's all a question of organisation Mum,' said Derek picking up the chant.

'You must be able to see the checkered flag by now,' said Anthony.

'So how are you going to fill your time on the home-stretch?' asked Martin later, addressing my backside half under his bed as I cleared out the apple cores, dirty socks and windsurfing magazines.

What they don't know God is that I'm about to keep the first of my New Year resolutions and throw the switch on their life-support machines, ie the stereo, the video machine, the phone and the Nescafé jar.

Audrey

Tuesday 2nd January

Dear God,

Tom announced at lunch, on this the eighth day of Christmas, that he wasn't going to waste his time learning the names of his sons' girl friends who flit in and out of the rectory, until he has to read their banns. He's got a point there because they're legion.

I used to greet each one at the front door as a potential daughter-in-law and emotionally exhaust myself making the necessary adjustments, but no longer God.

Anthony keeps throwing me though. He will follow me into the kitchen and, out of earshot of the current girlfriend, declare, 'This is *the* one Mum, believe me.' And once again I start down the track of looking at a potential member of the family, projecting myself into the future with all the necessary adjustments I'd have to make to cope with eg Tina's voice, Karen's nose stud or Julie's grape, walnut and cheese diet.

Audrey

Wednesday 3rd January

Dear God,
   On the ninth day of Christmas Tom asked the boys at breakfast if, before they returned to their halls of higher learning, they'd let him have his socks back.

Audrey

Thursday 4th January

Dear God,
   Today, the tenth day of Christmas, a new kitchen floor was put down at St Jude's rectory. The workmen mentioned that they'd laid one at St Bede's rectory last week so I was able to get the lowdown on Father Gary's and Debbie's other improvements.
   How they managed to squeeze a new kitchen out of the diocese complete with Laura Ashley tiles I don't know God. I'd heard rumours of course, but you can never be sure. What's more they've managed to wangle a front porch too; something about your rain falling on good and bad alike, but they, Gary and Debbie, weren't going to get wet.
   They must have also been talking to the bishop's wife who told me, 'If you don't get the rectory sorted out at the beginning my dear, you never will.'

Audrey

Friday 5th January

Dear God,

On the eleventh day of Christmas the rectory had it's first tramp. I always know they're at the door because Martin says, 'Mum, there's a gentleman at the door,' otherwise he'll shout, 'Mum, there's a man at the door.' He's full of positive discrimination is Martin.

Our tramp turned out to be a vegan so I had some difficulty finding him something nutritious to eat. He finally settled for baked beans on toast, three bananas and a bottle of ginger beer which he drank with his eyes fixed disapprovingly on my leather shoes.

Audrey

Saturday 6th January
The Epiphany of Our Lord

Dear God,

On the twelfth day of Christmas my true love said to me, 'Who's been using my blankety blank razor again?' His halo is slipping God. Is this ministry burnout or are there too many chiefs and too few Indians around?

Derek returns to his garret tomorrow, Anthony to his love nest and Martin retreats into Armageddon. All will be normal again.

Took down the Christmas cards, put away the decorations and vacuumed up all the pine needles. Christmas has come and gone. Was it just another Christmas of frenzied spending and overeating or has it been as Tom asks in his letter in the January magazine:

'A celebration of the Event, the unique Event; Jesus Christ, the Son of God, made man? An event which is at the centre of history, at the centre of the world, and at the centre of humanity–Jesus Christ, who, when we go to a quiet place and shut out the incessant noise and activism of the world, we find through silence and meditation at the centre of our lives. Jesus Christ, who broke into history two thousand years ago in a stable in Bethlehem to reveal the love of the Father, of which he himself is a sign. Jesus Christ, who came to reveal God's plan by which we are to become the Father's adopted sons through him and be gathered into one people, one church?'

Was it just another Christmas? I don't know God. Of course there was the usual last minute rush and panic, but there was also that mystical moment at the midnight service in the last verse of 'In the Bleak Midwinter' when we sang:

> What can I give him
> Poor as I am?
> If I were a shepherd
> I would bring a lamb,
> If I were a wise man
> I would do my part:
> Yet what I can I give Him–
> Give my heart.

But the church year moves on and today is the Feast of the Epiphany when the Wise Men following the star found Jesus in Bethlehem. Were they the pioneers of their day in seeking the meaning of life?

Audrey

Tuesday 9th January

Dear God,
   My predecessor left this poem on the inside of the rectory door:

> This may be the tenth or eleventh knock
> And the day isn't half way through,
> But remember before you sigh and groan
> That God's always there for you.

And someone, not a million miles away, has recently added in red felt tip underneath, 'Remember, God loves a cheerful door opener.'

By the way God, talking about Martin, you know he has this Saturday job at Tesco stacking pet food as he wants to buy a wet suit? Well, could you possibly get him transferred to another section because his conversation has been reduced to the relative merits and sales of Chum, Chappie and Pal; how most cats really prefer Whiskas and that the sale of flea collars rises with the temperature.

How about the baking section? There's not much one can say about a bag of flour or a tin of baking powder – though no doubt Martin will rise to the occasion. I think I'd better go to sleep after that God!

Audrey

Wednesday 10th January

Dear God,

Once again we're back to peace and quiet and Sammy following me around with an accusing look as if I'd engineered it all.

Drove Derek to the station this morning loaded with his Christmas spoils of war, plus one bath mat, one lavatory brush, two cushions and four Esso garage sherry glasses. This is serious nest making.

This afternoon I took Anthony back to his residence. Helped him carry his new term's rations up to the third floor where I was introduced to Leigh Ann and Julie camped outside his door. Obviously they'd seen from the bonfires on the hilltops that he was on his way.

Audrey

Thursday 11th January

Dear God,
   My husband's workplace is falling down. The stonework's crumbling, the roof slates are stricken with nail-sickness, the spire's wonky, the wiring's lethal and the choir stalls are held together by deathwatch beetles holding hands to keep warm because the heating's on the blink.

Audrey

Sunday 14th January
Epiphany 2
Theme: Revelation—The First Disciples

Dear God,
   St Jude's was 'done' last night. They took the bishop's chair, an antique flageolet from the glass case, the silver candlesticks and signed the visitors' book

Burglers'.

   During the intercessions this morning Tom prayed that the perpetrators be turned from their wicked ways and that we forgive them.
   At coffee afterwards the consensus was that they be boiled in oil.

Audrey
PS   Mother said that in her day even burglars could spell.

Monday 15th January

Dear God,

Behold, I tell you a mystery. You know how Tom and I say we like to get away from it all on a Monday, then why do we end up looking at other churches with a bite at a pub in between?

We check out which service they follow, which hymn book they use, and their tradition by reading the notice board. Predominance of mattins and they're low, predominance of communion and they're middle of the road, but predominance of communion, reserved sacrament and lace on the cottas in the vestry and they're high. Then, before we leave, we have a good read of their magazine – always a mine of information. It's all so fascinating.

I wonder God if there are other priests and their wives popping in and out of St Jude's on their day off too.

Audrey

Friday 19th January

Dear God,

I have no Christian courage. Had a tooth out this morning and nearly drowned in bits of tooth, amalgam, blood, cotton wool swabs and beads of perspiration from Mr Nash's brow.

I was holding on fine with all that deep breathing from child bearing years, until the crown of the tooth separated from its roots and Mr Nash bellowed down the passage to his partner, 'Root extractors, please.' I blacked out. Couldn't he have sent those dreaded words secreted in a note with the blonde nurse?

I feel I've let the whole side down – Tom, St Jude's, the Church of England and the Christian faith.

Of course, I wouldn't have passed out if I'd been gazing

up at his degree certificate (cum laude) pasted on the ceiling, with a distinction in extractions and a report from his professor on his steadiness of hand, instead of all those mobiles of Victoria Plum, Thomas the Tank Engine and Paddington Bear in that ridiculous hat.

Audrey

Saturday 20th January
Fabian, Bishop of Rome and Martyr

Dear God,
   Had a lovely day of 'tender loving care' today. Tom insisted that I get up late, that I keep warm, that he did the shopping, that the ironing could wait, that Martin take Sammy for his walk and that he'd get Mother to cook the dinner.
   Have just done an inventory of my teeth. Have twenty-eight left so look forward to many more days of TLC.

Audrey

Sunday 21st January
Epiphany 3
Theme: Revelation – Signs of Glory

Dear God,
   All TLC gone out of the window. Alarm failed to go off and was dragged out of bed by Tom to iron a clerical shirt and a cotta ten minutes before the 8.00am Eucharist.

Audrey

Wednesday 24th January
Francis de Sales, Bishop, Teacher, 1622

Dear God,

Mother dropped in on her way back from Sainsbury's and disgorged the contents of two carrier bags onto the kitchen table.

Martin says she's the 'good fairy' who saves clergy families from scurvy, rickets and kwashiorkor and that I mustn't knock her.

I don't God, it's just that she thinks mince on a Sunday is living below the bread line.

Audrey

Thursday 25th January
The Conversion of St Paul

Dear God,

Had Father Gary's wife, Debbie, around for coffee. She says Father Gary has his whole parish on a computer. He knows the state of play in each family–names, ages, who's baptised, who's confirmed, who's shacking up with whom, who's not talking to whom–jobs, pets, where they took their last holiday and details of their last operation. Before he goes visiting he just throws it all up on the screen and runs off a print-out.

I won't pass this on to Tom till tomorrow because he's had a heavy day.

Audrey

Sunday 28th January
Epiphany 4
Theme: Revelation: The New Temple

Dear God,
   It's Education Sunday and Wally Burt's turn to do the intercessory prayers. His prayers mesmerise me; they're so interwoven with overdone metaphors. Not much he can do with the subject of education I thought, but he did God. Oh yes, he did.
   1) We pray for all who are learning to love you.
   2) We pray that our leaders may grow in knowledge and understanding.
   3) Help us to know as the test paper of life unfolds before us, no matter how difficult the questions may seem, you are with us.
   4) We ask you to forgive us where we have made mistakes and blotted the foolscap of our lives.
   5) We pray for those for whom the book of life has closed, who have put down their pens and gone home.
   Well God, 'education' was a challenge, but I think he passed, don't you? The problem was that during the rest of the service I was doing mental gymnastics trying to go one better than Wally Burt.

Audrey

Tuesday 30th January
Charles I, King, Martyr, 1649

Dear God,
   Class three from our Church of England Junior School visited St Jude's today armed with clipboards headed 'St Jude's, our Parish Church'.
   They drew and labelled the pulpit, the font, the rood screen, (which of course they spelt 'rude'). They drew the

misericords, the stained glass windows and the lectern which at St Jude's sports a very handsome eagle to support the Bible.

They were told that the altar is the most sacred part of the church and is usually positioned at the east end and candles remind us that Christ is the Light of the World.

They learnt that St Matthew is represented by a winged man, St Mark by a winged lion, St Luke by a winged ox, St John by an eagle and St Peter by two crossed keys.

They learnt that the sign of a fish was originally a secret sign used by the early Christians when they were being persecuted and that the initial letters of the Greek words for 'Jesus Christ, Son of God, Saviour' spell the Greek word for 'fish'–hence the symbol of a fish representing Christianity. This really caught their interest.

They were told what the different liturgical colours stood for and learnt that the Bible is not just one book but many divided into two parts: the Old Testament and the New Testament.

At 11 o'clock it was biscuits and orange squash at the rectory, then back to St Jude's with Tom describing a typical day of a rector or vicar.

Then came the questions: do you get paid lots of money?; what do you wear underneath your robes? (today Tom and Jerry underpants.); have you ever seen God?; where does all the money go that people put into the collection bags?

These were followed by their comments: my granny's gone to heaven; my guinea pig's gone to heaven; it's my birthday and I got a mountain bike.

One little girl read a passage from the Bible at the lectern and two boys lit the altar candles with a taper and put them out with the snuffer.

They were interested, they were busy and before they went home Tom sat down at the organ and they all sang, 'Morning has Broken'. Most of them don't go to Sunday School and when they grow up will probably not go to church, but I hope they'll regard St Jude's as their parish church and, even if they only visit it occasionally, will feel more comfortable in it.

Audrey

Thursday 1st February

Dear God,
   Had the grave digger in for coffee this morning. He'd been hacking away at the frozen ground in the churchyard preparing the final resting place for Emily Jane Stone tomorrow and needed a bit of a rest.

Audrey

Friday 2nd February
The Presentation of Christ in the Temple

Dear God,
   Emily Jane Stone was buried to the left of the yew tree in St Jude's churchyard this morning. She was ninety-seven years old. No one at St Jude's can recall her, but according to the executor of her will she'd been a servant at the rectory many years ago and a faithful member of St Jude's before she moved away.
   With no living friends or relatives about, the church-wardens decided they should be there together with Doris Stubbs bearing a lovely wreath of carnations and chrysanthemums she'd put together from St Jude's.
   Present too were her executors and of course the funeral directors and Tom and myself, all of us with the same desire that she should not be alone at her end. If there were to be an award for the best undertakers, those in our area would certainly be in the running.

I've just begun to realise God what an important ministry the undertaker has. He is with the bereaved at the most sensitive time of their lives. He is often the first person to follow the doctor into the home of the deceased, meeting the relatives and friends who are very often shocked and bewildered.

It is the undertaker who with care, patience and sensitivity has to turn the minds of the family to thoughts of the funeral. Is it to be a burial or cremation? Is there to be a service in church? When and where is it to take place? What about the family from afar? What will be needed in the way of transport? Such details are difficult to think about in those first days of bewilderment and shock.

It is the undertaker who will have the task of taking away the body and of liaising closely with the minister who is to conduct the funeral. He will have to ensure that any legal matters are handled quickly and with minimum distress to the bereaved. And together with all this the undertaker needs to listen, comfort and be a source of strength for the bereaved. Yes God, their's is indeed a ministry.

Audrey

Sunday 4th February
Epiphany 5
Theme: Revelation – The Wisdom of God

Dear God,
By the time we'd reached the offertory hymn this morning I knew exactly what each person in the row behind me had left on auto cook for their Sunday lunch. Roast lamb and beef accompanied by roast potatoes, peas, carrots and Brussel sprouts jockeyed for first place. Blackberry and apple tart led the pudding field, with 'a nice bit of rhubarb' coming a close second.

The pew in front were into hip replacements. It seems that the Anglican Church runs on plastic joints.

At first I got mad. Then I felt bad about being mad and gave thanks for their 'togetherness'. Then I gave thanks that they all had enough to eat and for the great advances in medical science. Finally I said 'sh' and three woolly hats turned around in hurt surprise.

Audrey

Tuesday 6th February
The Queen's Accession (1952)

Dear God,

The boiler in the church has finally gone. Icicles hang from the communion rail and the congregation has halved. The bottom line says £20,000. A frenzy of jumble sales and fairs crowd into my diary.

Please God, let us find a crock of gold in the churchyard.

Audrey

Friday 9th February

Dear God,

Woke up this morning feeling rather down. Maybe I'm suffering from that lack of light syndrome, you know the thing you get around this time of the year when you haven't had enough sun.

But deep down I know it's more than that God. I know it's because I've let the ordinary nuts and bolts of living in a rectory take over. I've let the busyness of it all keep me from regular daily prayer and from the midweek communion for the past few weeks. My mind has been flooded with distractions at the Sunday Eucharist too, setting me adrift from you, which always means conflict for me.

It's a paradox isn't it God? Here I am, the wife of a priest living on the job and yet I can so easily be out of touch with you.

Audrey

Sunday 11th February
Ninth Sunday before Easter
Theme: Christ the Teacher

Dear God,

Tom has just come in from evensong. Says the congregation has doubled.

Some old chap spent the entire service quite astounded, watching Tom's every move. He told Tom at the door afterwards that he'd heard there'd been some changes going on in the Catholic church, but hadn't realised how many.

Tom says he won't tell him just yet that the Romans are on the same side but a block further down because he's enjoying the hundred percent increase.

Audrey

Tuesday 13th February

Dear God,

Tom won the 'funniest hat' competition at the Mothers' Union meeting today. Says it helps if he reminds himself that while he's being bored he's also being paid.

Audrey

Thursday 15th February

Dear God,
   Martin's friend Dale is ill. Martin says he's been off college now for about four weeks. It's something to do with his blood and he's to have a bone marrow transplant if they can find a match. It doesn't sound at all good. I wonder if Martin realises how serious it is?

Audrey

Saturday 17th February

Dear God,
   Tom says there's a subterranean mumbling coming from the first few pews and would I track it down tomorrow.

Audrey

Sunday 18th February
Eighth Sunday before Easter
Theme: Christ the Healer

Dear God,
   I've tracked it down. It's Mr Nutall. He's making a protest. He's following the 1662 Prayer Book while the rest of us are following the Alternative Service Book.

Audrey

PS   Mother says she won't take the cup from a homosexual and she can tell.

Tuesday 20th February

Dear God,

Am I experiencing a mid-life crisis? Today I put the milk in the oven and the post in the microwave. Mind you I've felt it coming on for some time now, ever since I realised that our new doctor is young enough to be my son and that by the time Martin leaves home I'll be too old to go on a kidney machine.

Who am I God? Am I the ever smiling beige coloured woman behind the tea urn every Sunday, or the middle-aged woman gyrating around the rectory kitchen to Chubby Checker's 'Let's Twist Again'? Am I the woman at the end of the phone with, 'Good morning, St Jude's rectory. May I help you?' Or am I the woman saving up from the house-keeping to have her hair streaked?

Why do people think that because I'm the rector's wife I've got it all sewn up–the meaning of life and you God? Don't they realise I'm like them, 'With many a conflict, many a doubt, Fightings within and fears without?'

Of course it's easier for camels, that's why they wear that supercilious look.

Audrey

Thursday 22nd February

Dear God,

Sammy had a heart attack this morning. He's very weak. The vet has doubled his pills, but says that if he doesn't improve we should think about putting him to sleep. Oh God, not Sammy.

Audrey

Friday 23rd February
Polycarp, Bishop of Smyrna, Martyr, c 155

Dear God,
   Sammy tried to come upstairs this morning for his usual
cuddle and rich tea biscuit, but only got halfway. Spent the
day on his beanbag in front of the fire.

Audrey

Saturday 24th February
St Matthias, Apostle and Martyr

Dear God,
   Sammy is worse. I've just phoned the vet. He says that we
have to make the decision, but that if it were his dog...
   Oh God, have we the right to end his life? Will we be
playing you God? But is it right to let him suffer? Why can't I
turn to the Bible and find the right answer?

Audrey

Sunday 25th February
Seventh Sunday before Easter
Theme: Christ the Friend of Sinners

Dear God,
   You understand. I just couldn't go to church this morning.
I've been waiting for a miracle all day and so has Martin.
Anthony came this morning and sat with Sammy stroking his
head and Derek phoned this evening to see if there'd been
any improvement. Since they were little children Sammy has
been there with them.

Tom and I dug his grave near the azaleas. We know we can't let him suffer any longer.

Audrey

Monday 26th February

Dear God,
Samuel Smudge, our darling Sammy, is dead. While I held his big black head, Tom held me. We didn't hear the vet drive away. We just cried and stroked him for a while then carried him on his beloved beanbag over to the azaleas and gently lowered him into the ground.

Where is he now God? Where is all that love, unquestioning loyalty and fun? Our bishop says he can't conceive a heaven where there's no Mozart and neither can I where there's no Sammy.

Do we transfigure that which we love, God?

Audrey

Tuesday 27th February
George Herbert, Priest, Pastor, Poet, 1633

Dear God,
Didn't sleep much last night. Had a huge hole inside me and after Martin left this morning an emptiness closed in on the rectory. Pooky can't fill the void. He's always lived on the edge of our lives, a black streak on the periphery of our vision. Sammy it was who held sway at ground level, which relegated Pooky to a higher plane, ie on top of the fridge, stove, washing machine, chair backs, window sills and in the sun on the bonnet of the car.

It's the beginning of Lent tomorrow and I haven't decided

yet what my Lenten penance should be. When I was nine I gave up sugar in tea which turned into forever. Do you think chocolate could turn into forever? But then if I gave up chocolate my motives would be mixed, ie suffering/getting into last year's skirts. Do I really want to give up Twix, Double Decker and Boosts with the danger of 'forever'?

Tom said in his sermon last Sunday that taking something on could be harder than giving something up. I could stop avoiding Mrs White at coffee on Sunday and give myself up to a half hour litany of symptoms, operations and treatments. She lives alone and really just wants to share her problems with someone. I could also give up being so critical and judgmental. God, I wish I could just be nicer!

I see from my diary that we remember George Herbert today. Must read his wonderful poem 'Love bade me welcome'. It always lifts me when I'm feeling down.

Audrey

Wednesday 28th February
Ash Wednesday

Dear God,

At 9.30am Miss Willis brought my Lenten penance around. Would I take the minutes at the Parochial Church Council meetings for the next six months while the secretary is overseas?

This is a terrible penance for me God. I avoid PCC meetings like the plague and what I hate most about them is listening to the boring old minutes being read! Chocolate would have been much easier or even Mrs White's operations. I had to say yes and have been suffused by a warm glow of martyrdom/saintliness all day.

But God, on this first day of Lent I did manage an hour of peace and stillness. I plan to make a space each morning for a quiet time. I will try to switch off from the parish, the washing and Martin's bedroom. Then, by the time Martin arrives home, I will be serene and calm and ready for anything he or the world can throw at me. This Lent it will be different.

Went to the Ash Wednesday service tonight with the imposition of ashes. 'Remember that you are dust, and to dust you shall return. Turn away from sin and be faithful to Christ,' said Tom as he made the sign of the cross in ash on our foreheads.

Audrey

Thursday 1st March
David, Bishop, Patron Saint of Wales, c 601

Dear God,

It's all gone, the peace I mean, and it's only the second day of Lent. Tonight I let rip at Martin when he spread half a jar of crunchy peanut butter on two slices of bread, and at Tom this morning when he asked me if I'd remembered to mend the hem of his alb.

Held our first Lenten study group at Major and Mrs Crabtree's home this evening. The theme this year is 'Onwards together'. It ended in chaos when we got to 'transubstantiation'. 'But that's what the Romans believe!' they cried.

Audrey

Friday 2nd March
Chad, Bishop of Lichfield, Missionary, 672

Dear God,
   Had a big lump in my throat at the supermarket today

near the dog food. No more Chunky–beef, turkey, chicken or rabbit; no more Good Dog Choc Drops, no more Sam. Oh God, I miss him so much.

Audrey

Sunday 4th March
First Sunday in Lent
Theme: The King and the Kingdom – Temptation

Dear God,
   The Sunday school children have dredged up their sins and stuck them on a big board at the back of the church.

   Mother says she blames it on the schools and the Bishop of Durham.

Audrey

Monday 5th March

Dear God,
   Went to the garden centre today and bought an orange azalea to plant on Sammy's grave–a new flame coloured strain called Brightest and Best.

Audrey

Tuesday 6th March

Dear God,
   After all the years of his father's nagging, ie 'electricity doesn't grow on trees', 'the house looks like a power station', 'don't have a bath up to your neck', etc, Derek has seen the light. It came in a blinding flash this morning with the postman in the shape of an electricity bill.
   He was on the phone straightaway with a strangled crack in his voice and I'm glad I was there at the other end to put him back together again. I was able to reassure him that all was in order, that they hadn't sucked 'standing charges' out of the air, that yes, his Mum and Dad had been getting electricity bills for years, and even if one has been living on cold baked beans and Coke for the last few months, no, I didn't think the European Court of Human Rights would be interested.
   Tom says I might regret suggesting he share a bath with a friend!

Audrey

Thursday 8th March
Edward King, Bishop of Lincoln, Teacher, Pastor, 1910

Dear God,

Held the second Lenten Study Group tonight. Started off discussing 'the Fruits of the Spirit.' Tom lost control halfway as the group split into two, one half discussing the new Sainsbury's and the other half the way the traffic rushes through the High Street.

Audrey

Friday 9th March
Ember Day

Dear God,

Tom is not an overly sensitive man, but if the blue tits decide to give his nesting box a miss again this spring he will take it as a personal insult. He spent his whole lunchtime yesterday carefully positioning his box in the rectory garden. So please God, see what you can do.

Audrey

Sunday 11th March
Second Sunday in Lent
Theme: The King and the Kingdom–Conflict

Dear God,

Had a visiting preacher this morning–Father David from St Mary's team ministry. His sermon was punctuated with long silences, or rather his long silences were punctuated with bits of sermon. I kept wondering if he'd forgotten what he was going to say. It was most nerve-wracking and I leant forward willing him to remember.

Why do I feel responsible for the whole show: for my husband and his performance each Sunday and visiting preachers too?

Father David's longest silence came just before the end. Now I was certain he had forgotten. Then, after an eternity, which he spent with his eyes closed and his face turned heavenwards while the congregation fiddled with their hearing aids or looked for the next hymn, he suddenly sprang to life, leaned over the pulpit and, with eyes boring into each one of us, said, 'And I quote you again those words from St Matthew's Gospel, "But he who endures to the end will be saved." '

We'd all been saved!

Audrey

Tuesday 13th March

Dear God,

Tom has retired to bed early with a migraine. Last time I looked in he'd assumed the foetal position. I blame it all on that article in *The Times* this morning, ie 'Vicar's life is no longer black and white'.

It seems that some clergy are into colour and image consultants. One cleric says he can't bring the 'good news' dressed in black and white, only in pink, turquoise or denim blue clerical shirts. Says he's in a 'spring flowing into summer' category and should wear light, bright, warm colours. It seems that evangelicals wear blue, anglo-Catholics black and liberals grey—a sort of holy colour discrimination.

Tom choked over his Sugar Puffs declaring that if they'd a diary like his they wouldn't have time to wonder whether they were 'spring flowing into summer', 'summer fading into autumn' or 'winter disappearing into death', and that he didn't aim to be user friendly. He then chomped through his toast and chocolate spread and barked that he was off to see Edith Thompson before she handed in her dinner plate.

Audrey

Wednesday 14th March

Dear God,

Listened to the 'Messiah' during my quiet time this morning. Ended up singing and conducting the whole thing. Felt quite exhausted by the time I reached 'Worthy is the lamb' and very guilty when the door bell rang and Kay Barber presented me with a contribution to the magazine which she said had taken her two hours to prepare.

I hope God that one gets Brownie points for making space in one's life for one of your greatest gifts, music, as well as for sweating over a report from the Mothers' Union for two hours.

Audrey

Thursday 15th March

Dear God,

Held our third Lenten Study Group tonight. From the start Tom took a firm hold on the group concentrating our minds on 'forgiveness'.

Mrs Hyde said she'd never forgiven her sister for not going to her mother's funeral, nor her father for forgiving her sister.

Major Crabtree said he would forgive everybody except the muggers of little old ladies who were beyond the pale.

Tom then said that 'forgiveness' was a bridge over which

all must cross, but was interrupted by Mrs Crabtree who asked if it were time to put the kettle on.

At the mention of tea three ladies disappeared into the kitchen and 'forgiveness' went out of the window.

Audrey

Sunday 18th March
Third Sunday in Lent
Theme: The King and the Kingdom – Suffering

Dear God,

Father Benton took over the reins at St Jude's today and Tom had the day off. By 9 o'clock we were on our way to the cathedral.

What joy to relax into a service without faces mouthing, 'See you about the jumble sale later,' or hands waving clutches of notices. What joy to be totally unaware of all the behind the scenes creaks and abrasions of ordinary human beings working together towards such a beautiful and seamless service.

I didn't know the people next to me, nor in front or behind, but still felt at one with them. But best of all God, Tom and I were together side by side in our worship; a rare and precious thing when your husband's a priest, and together we heard about the Kingdom of God.

After the last hymn 'Lord Jesus, think on me', we melted away anonymously into the cathedral precinct, into our car and back through the countryside stopping halfway for beef and horseradish sandwiches and half a bitter shandy.

It's been such a wonderfully refreshing day God.

Audrey

Tuesday 20th March
Cuthbert, Bishop of Lindisfarne, Missionary, 687
Thomas Ken, Bishop of Bath and Wells, 1711

Dear God,
    Had a letter from the rural dean this morning. He'd seen
Tom's letter in this month's magazine describing our
dilemma in having Sammy put to sleep. Says he's been
through it a few times himself and knows the anguish.
Wasn't that nice of him God?
    How can people say, 'I expect you'll get another dog?'
Nothing will ever replace Sammy.

Audrey

Wednesday 21st March
Thomas Cranmer, Archbishop of Canterbury, Martyr, 1556
Benedict, Abbot of Monte Cassino, 540

Dear God,
    Our first Annual Parochial Church Meeting at St Jude's
started with the reading of the minutes of the last annual
meeting, which was of course during the interregnum. It
seems that, without an incumbent, they'd all had a turn at
airing their grievances past and present.
    Tonight there were fourteen items on the agenda; the
most time consuming and mind bogglingly boring being item
4, the Treasurer's Report on the financial affairs of the
parish and 5, to receive the audited accounts of the PCC.
    Major Crabtree disappeared to the Dog and Duck for
'these, but with perfect timing, reappeared just in time for his
item, the Churchwardens' Report.
    By 10 o'clock Messrs Grimshaw, Grimshaw and
Grimshaw had been duly reappointed as auditors to the PCC
and thanked for their services during the last year.
    We were now on item 12, the rector's remarks. Here Tom

was brief and to the point—training from his business days when time meant money. We could be in bed by 11 o'clock if he hurried up I thought.

He took the opportunity to thank St Jude's for their support for himself and for his family and then proceeded to hit them between the eyes.

'The organ fund, the roof fund, the flower fund and the central heating fund are important and to all involved in fund raising activities for these we are deeply grateful, but these must not become an end in themselves—we are not a social club.

'We are at church for one reason only and that is to worship God. We must not lose sight of this in the activism that is so prevalent in the Anglican Church, and especially at St Jude's, where I sometimes think our patron saint should move over for Anneka Rice!

'Would a young person in search of God find what they wanted at St Jude's? Could they find a quiet centre beyond all the coffee mornings, fairs and jumble sales? Above all we must be that centre.'

We were now at item 13, date of first meeting of new PCC. With noses dipping into diaries this was soon settled.

'Any other business' asked Tom, gathering his papers together and hopefully tucking his pen back into his top pocket. Now the meeting began in earnest.

First Mrs Earnley stood up saying that the PCC should send a letter of thanks to Nellie Barber for the cushion she'd embroidered for the priest's chair in memory of Dick Soames, in spite of her bad legs.

Twenty minutes was spent on the fate of a redundant bookcase: should it be put in the jumble sale or taken apart and made into shelves for storing vases in the vestry.

Then Brenda said that the communion wine tasted of cough mixture, iron filings and old paint brushes (obviously been listening to Jilly Goolden on 'Food and Drink'), so she was asked to do some research at Oddbins and Bottoms Up and report back to the PCC at the next meeting. Hopes of being in bed by 11 o'clock had now faded.

Next came the resignation of Miss H. Patterson as sacristan at St Jude's. 'Much as I have enjoyed my nineteen years with all the different priests in the vestry,' she said, 'I feel I'm now beyond it and would like to hand over to someone younger.'

Then Tom got to his feet again, requesting that something be done about the six feet high weeds obscuring the driveway to the rectory. This immediately brought our botanist, Dr Forest, out of a long doze to his feet. 'The rector must be referring to the lovely Heracleum sphondylium of the umbellifer family,' he said. 'Hogweed, in plain English,' growled Major Crabtree.

Miss Flowers said it was lovely seeing so many meadow flowers growing in such profusion in one spot and that we mustn't add to the rape of the countryside with more careering lawn mowers. Miss Willis pointed out that the last time that piece of ground had seen a careering lawn mower was ten years ago.

By 11.45pm no decision had been made, except to put protectors around the three wild orchids nestling between the Heracleum sphondylium of the umbellifer family and the rest of the weeds.

Audrey

Thursday 22nd March

Dear God,

Held our fourth Lenten Study Group tonight. Tom spoke about the Eucharist being divided into four parts: adoration; contrition; thanksgiving; supplication, and that this was easy to remember because the first letter of each word formed the acronym ACTS.

Suddenly Miss Flowers became very excited saying, 'Well, there you are. There you are. Father was right. He was right.

He used to say "Primrose the facts are in the Acts, the facts are in the Acts." '

We all nodded sagely, desperately trying to make the connection.

Audrey

Saturday 24th March
The Annunciation of Our Lord to the Blessed Virgin Mary

Dear God,
'Behold, I am the handmaid of the Lord; let it be to me according to your word,' said Mary to the angel Gabriel when he told her she would bear a son. God, we are so far removed from the obedience of Mary today that we'd probably reply, 'It's not convenient at the moment', or 'What about my career structure?'

Today we run our own lives, we have rights, we have choices, we make our own decision, we are in charge, we live in a democracy, we *must* be happier–but are we?

God, you are an autocrat, not a democrat. Jesus didn't say, 'It's all right as long as it feels right for you,' or 'It's all right as long as you're not hurting anyone else.' You sent your Son to show us the way to that peace that passes all understanding, but it's not an easy option.

Audrey

Sunday 25th March
Fourth Sunday in Lent
Mothering Sunday
Theme: The King and the Kingdom – Transfiguration

Dear God,

Had the Sunday school in for the whole service this morning. Realised that most of the children were singing 'Give me joy in my heart keep me crazy' instead of 'keep me praising', going on with 'Give me joy in my heart I pray', which was all right until the third line, 'Give me joy in my heart keep me crazy', and the last line, 'Keep me crazy till the break of day'.

Tom delivered his sermon standing between the two front pews where the children were seated. The rest of the congregation took this as a signal that the rector was really talking to the children and they settled back with half shut eyes and patronising parental smiles on their faces.

About a quarter way into his sermon Tom advanced two paces up the aisle and in a loud voice said, 'Your parents think I'm only talking to you, but I'm also talking to them.' This brought Major Crabtree back from the wooden hills with a start and, grabbing a hymn book, he stood up.

At the end of the service trays of posies were brought in from the vestry and the children went up to collect one for their mothers, followed by some of we bigger children for our mothers. Then Tom, picking up the last posy, came down the aisle to where I was sitting and with a kiss gave it to me. Well God, the tears just welled up at this gesture, but also at the absence of even the youngest of the brothers Karamazov.

Martin was under the duvet when we got home, but a hand did come out and give me a card which read:

> My Mother is wonderful,
> My Mother is true.
> She's there when I need her,
> I wish I had two.

And on the front was a picture of a real bimbo.

Later, Derek phoned to say that he'd received an astronomical water bill, even though he hardly washes, and that he'd take them all to the European Court of Human Rights for charging so much for something that falls free from the heavens, and to wish me a happy Mother's Day.

Audrey

Tuesday 27th March

Dear God,

If we ever have another dog, and we won't, it would have to be a gold colour to match the lounge carpet. I'm still vacuuming Sammy's black hairs from the corners of the skirting boards. I feel quite treacherous.

It would have to be a female because they're more reliable when you take them out, and it would have to be a small dog as we're not getting any younger—that is, if we have another dog, and we won't.

Audrey

Wednesday 28th March

Dear God,

Felt so at peace after communion this morning. Sat in the churchyard on the bench given by Mrs Allanson in memory of her Arthur.

That's what I like about midweek communion: I can just slip out quietly afterwards and hold onto that peace a bit longer than is possible after the Sunday service.

Audrey

Thursday 29th March
John Keble, Priest, Pastor, Poet, 1866

Dear God,

At the fifth Lenten Study Group tonight we discussed the body of Christ; that we as that body are called to carry Christ's message and to reveal his love to the world, to show that even though we are weak, he is the priority in our lives.

But priorities were a little confused tonight God. Mr and Mrs Burt sent their apologies, they were having friends to dinner and Major Crabtree only appeared near the end, smelling strongly of the Dog and Duck.

Audrey

Friday 30th March

Dear God,

Dear, gentle Anne James has a malignant brain tumour. She's never married and has kept house for her father since her mother died. Her father keeps saying, 'I must be strong for Anne's sake,' and when Tom went round to see Anne yesterday, she asked him to pray with her for her father and for what lies ahead for both of them.

God, Anne is one of those quiet people who are so easily passed over in the noise and bustle of parish life, but who are the backbone of worship in the church; not only worshipping on a Sunday, but also with the two or three gathered together for the weekly communion too.

Audrey

Sunday 1st April
Fifth Sunday in Lent (Passion Sunday)
Theme: The King and the Kingdom; The Victory of the Cross

Dear God,

We heard today how Jesus Christ was condemned and put to death. He wasn't murdered by some thief or robber or hooligan on the rampage. He was crucified by the most righteous and respectable of the religious leaders under the authority of the Roman governor. All had a vested interest in his death. So why God are we so surprised and shocked today when the law catches up with the rich and powerful and 'respectable'?

Tomorrow, instead of visiting other churches we're going to do a round of the dog rescue homes in the area, just to have a look.

Audrey

Monday 2nd April
Commence Children's Society Family Week

Dear God,

She's a black Labrador/Springer Spaniel with a white chest, four white socks, a white tipped tail, Spaniel-like ears and legs that go on forever. Her name is Sally, she's ten months old and oh God, she's beautiful.

Of course she's going to be properly disciplined, none of this Good Dog Choc Drops lark. We've bought a new bean-bag and a book *Enjoy your Dog*. We'll be in control!

Audrey

Tuesday 3rd April
Richard, Bishop of Chichester, 1253

Dear God,
  During the night Sally chewed her way through the outer and inner covering of her beanbag, releasing thousands of small white Polystyrene beads. The rectory was awash and by lunchtime I was still gathering them up from behind the stove and under the fridge, proving that the sum of the parts can indeed be greater than the whole.

Audrey

Wednesday 4th April
Ambrose, Bishop of Milan and Doctor, 397

Dear God,
    By ten o'clock this morning Sally had eaten a sock, two paper napkins and one clothes peg complete with wire spring. I'm so worried she'll get a blockage. Tom says it's just high spirits.

Audrey

Thursday 5th April

Dear God,
    The last Lenten Study Group tonight was in the form of a 'Question and Answer' evening:

Question: Why do good people suffer as much as bad people?
Tom: I don't know.
Question: Do dogs go to heaven?
Tom: I'm not sure. Mine won't.
Question: What do you think of General Synod?
Tom: I try not to.

All agreed they had learnt so much and that there was still so much to learn. Ended by singing favourite hymns.
    A house plant was given to Major and Mrs Crabtree for the use of their home, who then let their two Rottweillers out of the kitchen to meet the group.

Audrey

Friday 6th April

Dear God,

Sally chewed the post this morning, including a cheque from the Society of the Blessed Virgin Mary for £25 for the hire of the hall. Tom had to write and ask for another. He says it's all a matter of discipline.

Audrey

Saturday 7th April

Dear God,

The rectory has its full complement once more. Anthony and Derek are home for Easter.

This afternoon I helped with the making of the palm crosses for tomorrow. After an hour I'd still not mastered this most complicated of holy crafts and volunteered to make tea for those who had instead.

Audrey

Sunday 8th April
Palm Sunday
Theme: The Way of the Cross

Dear God,

Our symbolic Palm Sunday walk into Jerusalem started at the duck pond. Tom and the choir, holding palms aloft, led the procession. The singing was launched with 'Ride on! ride on in majesty!'

By the end of the fourth verse the tail end of the procession was one verse behind the choir. We got cut in two

near the launderette, but managed to catch up at Rikky's Chippy. We were now on a different hymn to the choir.

I know God that this is witnessing, but I feel so self conscious walking in procession in public and then guilty for feeling so, but then you never did say that witnessing would be easy.

Audrey

Monday 9th April
Monday in Holy Week

Dear God,

Sally refuses to sleep on the floor and keeps climbing onto the chairs. Tom says the bottom line is discipline and that it's up to me as I'm with her all day.

Audrey

Tuesday 10th April
Tuesday in Holy Week

Dear God,

Tom and I went to the Blessing of the Oils service at St Peter's, Brighton, today. It was good to get out of the parish and to be with so many fellow clergy. There'd been a three line whip by the bishop this year, so they were all there in their robes.

As the oils of baptism, confirmation and healing were blessed, it felt so very ancient and right. The readings were from St Luke's Gospel:

> The Spirit of the Lord is upon me, because he has anointed me to preach good news to the poor. He has sent me to proclaim release to the captives and recovering of sight to the blind, to set at liberty those who are oppressed, to proclaim the acceptable year of the Lord (Lk 4:18-19).

and from St James:

> Is anyone among you suffering? Let him pray. Is any cheerful? Let him sing praise. Is any among you sick? Let him call for the elders of the church, and let them pray over him, anointing him with oil in the name of the Lord; and the prayer of faith will save the sick man, and the Lord will raise him up; and if he has committed sins, he will be forgiven (Jas 5:13-15).

I thought of the precious oils that Tom would take back with him to St Jude's; of Anne James who is dying and who Tom will anoint tomorrow and of baby Matthew James who will be baptised on Sunday.

All the priests sat together in the body of the church and when we came to the final hymn 'Shine Jesus, Shine' they nearly lifted the roof off.

Afterwards, before emerging into the noise of the town,

there was time to greet priests and their wives we'd been with at theological college–finding out how they were faring and hearing myself say, 'Yes, things are going well with us' and, 'Yes, we like our parish,' and at that moment, as the last strains of the organ died away, really meaning it. Yes, it is good to get away from the parish sometimes God.

Audrey

Wednesday 11th April
Wednesday in Holy Week

Dear God,
   Today Sally consumed another sock, one tea towel, one wipey, two more pegs and a plastic flower pot. I don't care if she gets a blockage. Why can't she be satisfied with her squeaky ball and plastic pork chop?
   Julie, one of Anthony's current girl friends, has moved into the rectory for the Easter weekend. Maybe they'd like to take Sally for some long walks.

Audrey

Thursday 12th April
Maundy Thursday

Dear God,
   Nearly two thousand years ago tonight you said, 'Do this in remembrance of me' and this command has been obeyed ever since.
   I have come to the communion rail in joy, in grief, in gratitude, in fear, for comfort, for strength, for forgiveness; to give thanks when the children were born, when loved ones

were ill and when Dad died, when exams were passed; in confusion, in doubt, on behalf of others and for myself.

From the opening sentence, Jesus said, 'A new commandment I give to you, that you love one another; even as I have loved you.' Tom's sermon put the emphasis on love and service. This was followed by the Washing of Feet while the choir sang 'Ubi Caritas'.

This was a first for St Jude's and the whole congregation physically leaned forward as Tom knelt down to wash and dry the feet of six parishioners–Harry our gardener, Joan who has learning difficulties, Mr and Mrs Barnes, Doris Stubbs and Michael from the choir.

Secondly, Tom emphasised the Institution of the Lord's Supper, and the slight change in the words for Maundy Thursday from, 'who in the same night that he was betrayed' to 'who in *this* night when he was betrayed' rolled back nearly two thousand years.

Then the altar coverings were removed, the candles extinguished and the altar cross covered in white linen.

There was no dismissal. In silence the congregation filtered out into the night while some made their way to the Lady Chapel to keep watch in turn till the dawn of Good Friday.

Audrey

Friday 13th April
Good Friday

Dear God,
   Every Good Friday kneeling we sing, 'See from his head, his hands, his feet, Sorrow and love flow mingled down'. Every Good Friday an overwhelming awareness floods through me of all the unconditional love and blessing I have received throughout all my life from you, through my family, through my friends. Every Good Friday I am brought face to face with myself as I am and when we sing, 'Love so amazing, so divine, Demands my soul my life my all', I am, for just that moment in time, changed. And so it was again today.

Audrey

Saturday 14th April
Easter Eve

Dear God,
   This evening we gathered outside the west door of a darkened St Jude's for the Service of Light–the blessing of the new fire and the lighting of the Easter candle.
   Tom lit the candle with a taper lit from a small bonfire saying, 'May the light of Christ, rising in glory, banish all darkness from our hearts and minds.'

We moved into St Jude's, stopping inside the porch while the Gospel was read by the light of the candle. Tom then raised the candle with the acclamation, 'The Light of Christ,' and the congregation responded, 'Thanks be to God.' The light moved further into St Jude's and two more stops were made with the same acclamation and response.

Then we lit our small individual candles, first from the Easter candle and then from one to another. Here was the Light of Christ spreading through St Jude's bringing to life its stone walls. Here was Christ, the Light of the World, risen from the darkness of the grave.

Finally, the Easter candle was placed in a stand on the chancel steps with the acclamation, 'Alleluia. Christ is risen.' And our response, 'He is risen indeed. Alleluia.' We then made our first Communion of Easter. Love had come back into the world.

St Jude's is all ready and waiting for you tomorrow God – a mass of daffodils and Easter lilies. The brass work gleams and the pews exude a faint scent of lavender polish. Doris Stubbs allowed me, under her beady eye of course, to arrange the flowers in the pedestal for the chancel steps.

Tom has just put the finishing touches to his sermon and the boys are busy protesting that, as God loves us just as we are, what's wrong with their jeans and trainers for tomorrow's service. When I retired to bed they were busy swapping ties, so there's hope.

Audrey

PS   I predict a mad scramble for the bathroom tomorrow morning. Julie has just hijacked the bathroom for two hours.

Sunday 15th April
Easter Day

Dear God,
   As predicted there was a mad scramble for the bathroom this morning, aggravated by the fact that Julie had to wash her hair just once more half an hour before the service.
   The Carter family weren't able to make their entrance together as Martin, being last in the queue for the hair-dryer, arrived late. He arrived in the middle of the processional hymn 'Hail Thee Festival Day' and got himself entangled with the flow of clergy, choir, candles and servers near the main door.
   But it was so good to be all together in church for once, even if an amazing assortment of ties above belied the size twelve trainers resting on the kneelers below. Julie had dressed entirely in black for the occasion with lipstick, eye shadow and nail polish to match!
   Just before the offertory hymn I committed, according to my sons, the most gross act any mother could. I doled out collection money to them. Well, they didn't have any did they?
   Tom spoke about new beginnings and I hoped his sons were listening, though taking a sideways glance at one point I doubted Anthony was, as he and Julie made cow eyes at each other.
   Later, over the Sunday roast, the three of them set upon Tom's sermon and tore it to shreds. They'd actually been listening God! What joy! How dare they!
   After dinner quiet descended on the rectory as we all curled up with our Easter eggs and the Sunday papers. By tea time two of us had chocolate headaches.
   It's been a very good Holy Week and Easter for me God; my first at St Jude's. I think it's been good for Tom too, in spite of all the hard work and tension that goes into the preparation and execution of so many important services, each one a public performance.
   God, you know how Tom and I pray for the boys. I know

we can't be the author of their lives, but please help them to come to know you more. They're hectic, but they're fun and we love them so much.

Audrey

Tuesday 17th April
Tuesday in Easter Week

Dear God,
   Had a little sit in St Jude's this afternoon, so peaceful and still fragrant with the flowers from Sunday. Had a little weep, not sure why, maybe for Anne James. God, if she has to die this way, let it be quick and surround both her and her father with your strength and love.
   I know that just because one is a Christian one is not spared what other people suffer, but it's so hard when bad things happen to such good people.

Audrey

Thursday 19th April
Thursday in Easter Week

Dear God,
   I'm worn out. Before breakfast that Labrador/Springer started by chewing half the post again, followed by another tea towel and a Marks and Spencer's bag. I've had to relent and buy Good Dog Choc Drops to coax the contents of the rectory out of her mouth. She always comes to show us her latest spoil, with her tail wagging furiously and her bright eyes saying, 'catch me if you can!', but the slightest move on my part towards her and she darts away.
   Tom says she's completely out of control and that it's all a

matter of discipline. I hope she gets a blockage and I hope he does too if he mentions 'discipline' again.

Audrey

Saturday 21st April
Saturday in Easter Week

Dear God,
   Anthony was driven back to residence this morning by Leigh Ann who's just been given a car by daddy for her eighteenth birthday. Derek got the 2.10pm train back to Kev and Mandy.
   There's still a week to go before St Jude's annual jumble sale, but we can't move in the rectory for books, pots, pans, crockery, stringless tennis racquets, cushions, faded pictures and masses of black bin bags stuffed full of clothes.
   Sally's had a field day with a thousand different smells to be sniffed and new delights to be dragged through the rectory and around the garden.
   I feel we've been invaded by the great unloved, unwashed and unimaginable. Can't wait till next Friday when it all goes over to the hall to be sorted and priced.

Audrey

Sunday 22nd April
Easter 1 (Low Sunday)
Theme: The Bread of Life

Dear God,
   Miss Flowers fainted halfway through Tom's sermon this morning. Before you could say 'ecumenical' four bottles of

smelling salts appeared under her nose and four good men and true bore her down the aisle into the fresh air.

That put paid to Tom's sermon which had taken him four hours to prepare.

Audrey

Tuesday 24th April

Dear God,
   'People look so miserable when they come out of church,' said Martin over his toast and syrup this morning.

I suppose St Jude's isn't what you'd term a 'lively' church, but I hope we're not miserable! I've been to 'lively' services where I've been swept up in the sheer energy and warm affirmation of faith and I've come out on a high. I've also been to services where I've entered into your presence through stillness, holiness and reverence and have come out in a more reflective mood.

I think it's good to experience both God.

Audrey

Wednesday 25th April
St Mark the Evangelist

Dear God,
   What's going on? When I tell people that Sally is a Labrador/Springer they roll their eyes. When I tell them she's a dog for our middle years they laugh. I feel they know something I don't.

Audrey

Thursday 26th April

Dear God,

Tom and I went to Burrswood today for their Thursday morning healing service. Because of roadworks we arrived one minute before the service began and fell out of the car into the chapel.

An absolute babble of thoughts flooded into my mind as I hastily tried to recall all the people and situations I'd wanted to bring to the service for your healing. I soon realised this was no good, so I sat back in my pew and picked up the service leaflet which said:

> Let us, by an act of will, place ourselves in the presence of our Divine Lord, and with an act of faith ask that he will empty us of all self and of all desire save that his most blessed will may be done, and that it may illumine our hearts and minds.
>
> We can then gather together all those for whom our prayers have been asked, and hold them silently up to Him, making no special request–neither asking nor beseeching–but just resting, with them, in Him, desiring nothing but that our Lord may be glorified in them.
>
> In this most simple way of approach He does make known his most Blessed will for us. For so he giveth Himself to his beloved in silence.

Afterwards, in that peace and silence Tom and I sat in the beautiful spring gardens.

Audrey

Friday 27th April

Dear God,

Carted all the jumble over to the hall this morning. What

a relief to have the rectory with its own indigenous smells to ourselves again. Tom's headache's beginning to clear.

Helped Madge Dunbar, Doris Stubbs, Miss Flowers and Kay Barber sort and price the jumble this afternoon. They've had years of experience, and it shows. Within an hour they'd sorted it all into various piles. The books had been examined for any first editions and the crockery, vases and ornaments for any stray pieces from the Ming Dynasty. They know that a cream coloured evening top, encrusted with sequins, would only fetch 50p, but that a faded blue denim skirt without a hem would fetch £1.

God, I've got a lot to learn. Maybe there should be training parishes for priest's wives too.

Audrey

Saturday 28th April

Dear God,

Today we held our spring 'rearrangement of the rubbish' (jumble sale). I was on books, so was able to have a good read after the initial scrum with the book dealers.

Memories of my total sex education came flooding back with a copy of 'Forever Amber'. Miss Willis bought it for her ninety-one year old mother who's resting up in bed with high blood pressure.

Halfway through there were still mounds of jumble left and I paled with rising panic as I pictured it all back at the rectory. Then Miss Flowers, as if reading my mind, suggested that for £1 we let them stuff a binbag with as much jumble as they could. You know God, I've been seriously underestimating Primrose Flowers. I'm beginning to think she's on my side.

Suddenly, idly 'picking over' turned into frenzied 'stuffing in' as the punters dashed from one pile of jumble to another shoving into their bin bags things they never knew they needed. Of course, I know that when they get home they'll realise they need a strapless rucksack or a lidless teapot like a hole in the head and it will all appear on the next jumble sale, but at least in the meantime it's being housed round the parish and NOT IN THE RECTORY!

Audrey

Sunday 29th April
Easter 2
Theme: The Good Shepherd

Dear God,
　　There are 'cat' congregations and there are 'dog' congregations. The 'cat' congregations venerate the building, purring over its history, ancient bricks and mortar, and rubbing their backs in ecstasy along the misericords. They don't care who's running the show as long as the venue stays the same.
　　The 'dog' congregations don't mind whether they're sitting on 12th century pews or on tubular steel and plastic stacking chairs, as long as the incumbent stays the same.
　　Either way there's a bit of idolatry going on!

Audrey

Monday 30th April

Dear God,
　　Tom's day off, but he had to attend a Deanery chapter meeting this morning–a sort of clergy 'get together'.
　　He came back quite elated. Seems he's not the only one who feels frustrated, isolated, inadequate, demoralised,

washed-up, overworked, lost, bullied, undermined and one hundred and one years old.

Audrey

Wednesday 2nd May
Athanasius, Bishop of Alexandria, Teacher of the Faith, 373

Dear God,

We have a flock of Soay sheep that graze the churchyard. They are lovely gentle creatures, but the congregation is divided about them. Some say it's sacrilege, others say it makes good economic sense. I say I'd love to have sheep lying on my grave and rubbing their woolly backs against my headstone.

They do make short work of fresh flowers though, so we keep them out over Christmas and Easter when people like to remember their loved ones.

Perhaps God you should take a Mori poll up there: 'Do you, or do you not, like sheep sleeping on your earthly remains?'

Audrey

Friday 4th May

Dear God,

Every morning I have to do a Zola Budd around the rectory garden in pursuit of Sally with something dangling from her mouth. This morning it was a pair of my tights, yesterday it was Tom's Tom and Jerry underpants. This evening she ate *Enjoy Your Dog*!

As Sally came from a litter of ten perhaps I do not suffer alone. Maybe I should trace the other owners; we could form a support group for each other while our dogs take the world apart!

Audrey

Sunday 6th May
Easter 3
Theme: The Resurrection and the Life

Dear God,

   Mrs Burt thinks Tom is psychic. She'd been explaining to me before the service this morning that she hadn't been the previous week because she'd had to plant her scarlet runners, but that anyway she felt one was nearer to God's heart in a garden.

   Later, Tom leaned over the edge of the pulpit and said, 'We are not nearer God's heart in a garden and neither,' he went on, 'are we nearer God's heart at the car boot sale taking place down the road at this very moment which has syphoned off a goodly section of St Jude's.'

   He ended his sermon (or ticking off) with a poem he'd seen on the wall of St Mary Magdalene, Launceston, Cornwall:

> On Sundays whether wet or fine,
> My church I always visit,
> So when at last I'm carried in
> The Lord won't say, Who is it?

I think it would be wise for Martin to keep the set of weights he picked up at the car boot sale under his bed for a while.

Audrey

Wednesday 9th May

Dear God,

Went to see Anne James this afternoon. She didn't recognise me—just sat there smiling. Her father says she doesn't appear to be in much pain. He looks very tired, but says he is being supported by all the prayers and kindness of the St Jude's people.

Wally Burt cuts their lawn, Madge Dunbar does their shopping twice a week, and young Michael from the choir walks their old dog. Doris Stubbs sees to their washing and ironing and many others help stock their freezer with little meals.

Forgive me God for all the hasty judgments I make about people, especially about Madge and Doris.

Audrey

Friday 11th May

Dear God,

I'm drowning in a sea of other people's expectations, eg 'I expect you're very busy; you're used to having an open house; you know everyone's name; you haven't a moment to spare.'

I'm consumed with guilt when I'm not busy, when the house is quiet, when I curl up with a book, when I forget a parishioner's name, when I sit down with a cup of tea, when I paint my nails and when I eat a whole box of Ferrero Rocher at one sitting.

Tom feels guilty when he has a minute to himself, when the phone and doorbell don't ring together, when he can't remember why Mrs Shaw has been missing from the front pew for six weeks, when he hasn't got two weddings on a Saturday and four services on a Sunday, and especially guilty when no one dies on his day off!

Audrey

Sunday 13th May
Easter 4
Theme: The Way, the Truth and the Life

Dear God,

Well of course it had to come. The noise level in St Jude's this morning prior to the 10.30am Eucharist was something awful. Five minutes before the service Tom took action. He erupted out of the vestry, climbed into the pulpit and said, 'Brethren, shall we collect ourselves.'

The reaction was one of complete disbelief. Eyes rolled, eyebrows rose and lips pursed. There was a general scurrying back to pews, leaving bits of church business and gossip unfinished. A silence followed unknown at St Jude's and the organist could be heard playing a Bach fugue.

I'd like to give Tom all the credit, but I can't. Ever since he'd heard that the Dean had chastised the cathedral congregation with those same words 'Brethren, shall we collect ourselves,' he's bided his time waiting for the right moment to use them on St Jude's.

Audrey

Monday 14th May
St Matthias the Apostle, Christian Aid Week

Dear God,

It's the beginning of Christian Aid week and I'm collecting in Church Road and Highbeech Close. Delivered all the envelopes this evening. Must remember that behind the letter slot at 12 Church Road there's a heaving, growling mass that dines on fingers.

Tom mowed the rectory lawns this morning and planted the Sedum plants Wally Burt gave us. Wally says we can't go wrong with them. What he doesn't know is that both Tom and I can kill a giant redwood with a glance.

This afternoon went for a long cross country walk with Sally—must have done at least five miles. Halfway we lay down on our backs between the long grasses, buttercups and ox-eyed daisies, letting the warm sun seep into us while St Jude's parish seeped out of us. Sally spent the time rushing from rabbit hole to rabbit hole getting rid of her excess energy.

I see from my diary that today is the feast day of St Matthias the Apostle. I never knew God that he was chosen after the Ascension to fill the vacancy in the Twelve left by the treachery of Judas Iscariot. It seems he'd been a follower of Christ from the beginning of his ministry.

Audrey

PS   Mother says she's not taking the cup from anyone with mascara and dangling ear-rings.

Tuesday 15th May

Dear God,

I'm quite excited. A loop system was installed at St Jude's this week. Just by moving a switch on their hearing aids to the T position, our deaf at St Jude's will be tuned to the system. Immediately all background noise will cease and they will be able to hear clearly what is being said at the altar, from the lectern and from the pulpit. This will affect many who haven't heard the sermon for years.

I've put up a notice in the porch with a big ear on it drawing attention to St Jude's wonderful new facility. I've also written an explanatory piece for this month's magazine extolling its virtues.

Of course, it's cost an arm and a leg and I had to lobby very hard to get the idea passed by the PCC. It was touch and go whether they'd agree.

The fact that the cathedral had one made no impression,

but letting drop that Father Gary's church had just had one installed seemed to make all the difference.

Audrey

Wednesday 16th May

Dear God,

Madge Dunbar told Tom yesterday that she doesn't want 'Rest in peace' on her tombstone, she wants 'Gone to higher service'. She says hell for her would be having nothing to do.

Why is it that the Madge Dunbars of this world make the rest of us feel so guilty? I was looking forward to the 'Resting in peace' and the 'Resting from one's labours' bit. I'm going to make a mid-year resolution not to feel so guilty. Tom says activism is the opiate of the Anglican Church.

Collected most of the Christian Aid envelopes this evening. Had an overwhelming desire to 'take out' 6 Highbeech Close who gave me back an empty envelope saying, 'If people get themselves into a mess they can get themselves out of the mess', and 28 Church Road who said, 'You don't know where the money goes, do you?'

I haven't the right temperament for the job God. I get so angry and find myself feeling the envelopes as I retreat down the path trying to differentiate between £1 coins and 1p and 5p pieces, or even buttons!

Audrey

Thursday 17th May

Dear God,

Went to St Bede's this evening for a joint confirmation service. We had nine candidates, St Bede's had twenty-three ranging from ten to eighty years. The gossip is that Father Gary prepares for confirmation anything that moves.

To the candidates the Bishop said, 'Even after all the preparation you have received in your confirmation classes and after all the prayer that has surrounded these preparations, for most of you it will be a great leap in faith. You should not feel guilty about doubts that assail you now and will in the future. The most important thing is your desire to be confirmed.'

One St Bede's mother had made a large square cake for the occasion, iced in luminous blue, bearing the names of their twenty-three candidates in red.

Jenna from our Sunday school was given a pair of large gold crosses for her newly pierced ears which brushed her shoulders. Tom predicted over an iced cup cake in St Bede's hall later that, by the time she was twenty her ear-lobes would resemble those of some African tribes.

Michael from our choir says he's been given a computer to remind him of his confirmation. Do I detect a bit of bribery here God?

It made a nice change to walk out of the hall at the end and leave all the cleaning up to someone else.

Audrey

Friday 18th May

Dear God,

Collected the balance of the Christian Aid envelopes this morning. Stopped for a coffee at 4 Highbeech Close with Mrs Burt. She's the source of those crocheted poodles that cover spare toilet rolls. She's already made a dozen for the Summer Fair.

Also had a chat with Mrs Jackson at 29 Church Road. Told me she's never been back to St Jude's since Father

George took leave of his senses one Easter morning and swung incense around.

Tom, rolling his eyes said, 'You win some, you lose some.'

Audrey

Saturday 19th May
Dunstan, Archbishop of Canterbury, 988

Dear God,

Derek was on the phone at lunchtime today demanding to know where all his 'me' years had gone. Said Kev and Mandy had sloped off this morning and left him to give the flat its quarterly clean up single handed. This gave him the opportunity to get on the phone and have a grumble about Kev and Mandy's lack of house training.

(1) Kev's never heard of bin liners; the neighbours have complained about the smell and he, Derek, has had to clean the whole disgusting mess out.

(2) Mandy drapes wet towels over everything even the pictures.

(3) Kev's girl friend Joanna eats all the cheese from the fridge and he, Derek, can't afford to live at that rate.

(4) Kev can't rinse out a coffee mug without flooding the kitchen floor and involving him, Derek, in the mopping up process.

(5) Mandy isn't vacuum cleaner, squeegee mop, or duster literate.

Well, I could really sympathise couldn't I God? But as for his 'me' years I couldn't help him there. Said I really didn't know what they were, but asked him to let me know if he ever found them because I'd like some too and, if they were what I thought they were, then I was still being robbed blind of them by Anthony and Martin. As for Kev and Mandy, I felt they were certainly having their 'me' years.

God, my children won't go. It's like getting chewing gum

off my fingers. Even if they're not physically with me, they're still attached by that umbilical cord called the telephone.

Why don't they tell me nice things, like how they've come out on their grant with a bit to spare, or how they're heading for a distinction and not about the gunge clinging to the sides of their dustbin?

On the plus side, this quarter's clean up has thrown up two jerseys he thought he'd lost, three odd socks he thinks belong to his Dad, and his 'You must be joking' T shirt he accused Anthony of stealing.

Audrey

Sunday 20th May
Easter 5 (Rogation Sunday)
Theme: Going to the Father

Dear God,
Our first Sunday with the loop system in place. Did some private research as to the reactions at coffee afterwards.

Asked Emily Potts, who's ninety-two, how she'd got on with it. 'I'm not bothered with it 'cause when you get to my age dearie you've heard them all,' she said. Oh God, I suppose she has.

When I finally got through to Maud Barber, she said that she never uses her hearing aid in church, only when she goes to bingo.

God, I think of Tom beavering away at his sermon each week, honing and polishing each word to drop into St Jude's ears and some of them are wilfully and literally SWITCHED OFF! I'm sure that's a sin, and if it's not, it should be. I'm fed up God. I want to shake them all!

I take it personally too. The loop system was going to be the mark I'd leave on St Jude's. My predecessor left behind a new Mother's Union banner, and Father Gary's wife is busy making a new altar frontal appliquéd with circles, triangles, railway lines and sunbursts which, when decoded, add up to the Holy Trinity. But my attempt to link our deaf members with the altar, the lectern, the pulpit and you God has failed. I don't think I'll make my findings known to the PCC.

Audrey

Tuesday 22nd May
Rogation Day

Dear God,
   Took Sally to the vet this morning. Yesterday she ate two pink plastic hair rollers and was in great pain. The vet says that if she's still in pain tomorrow it will be the full works– X-rays, anaesthetic and the knife.
   Please, please God don't let anything happen to her. She's so young and just full of life.

Audrey

Wednesday 23rd May
Rogation Day

Dear God,
   She's better. Ate all her breakfast, slept on the couch till lunch time, then dug up Tom's Spider lilies. I don't think they'll survive Sally. I don't think I'll survive Sally!

Audrey

Thursday 24th May
Ascension Day

Dear God,

I watch *Neighbours*. If I miss it at 1.30pm I catch it at 5.35pm.

Tom's daily fix is twenty minutes shut-eye in his chair after the lunchtime news. Mine is *Neighbours*. The story line is so simple that I can combine it with reading *The Times* or with a little doze. Keeping just half an eye open on auto-pilot I can still keep abreast of what's going on.

The only thing I can't do is tell anyone I watch it!

Audrey

Sunday 27th May
Sunday after Ascension Day
Theme: The Ascension of Christ

Dear God,

Salome Sabrina Jade Smith was baptised at St Jude's this morning supported by a baptismal party of at least forty strong. I felt sorry for them right in the front pews, standing when they should be sitting, sitting when they should be kneeling and no one in front of them to follow.

'Why are those men wearing frocks?' asked a little girl from the party when Tom came in with the servers. What I couldn't see was a small boy in the front pew with a pair of toy binoculars trained on Tom's every move.

'Never,' said Tom afterwards, 'have I ever felt so disconcerted in my whole life. It was like delivering a sermon to God, or worse still to Mrs Thatcher.'

The parents and godparents looked rather self-conscious at that part of the service when they were centre stage on the chancel steps with Salome Sabrina Jade.

Then Tom said, 'God has received you by baptism into his church.'

We, the body of Christ, responded, 'We welcome you into the Lord's Family. We are members together of the body of Christ; we are children of the same heavenly Father; we are inheritors together of the kingdom of God. We welcome you'.

Then, as is customary at St Jude's, the whole congregation clapped. I'm not sure about this clapping God, but it certainly put the parents and godparents at ease and they beamed broadly.

Of course, our regulars suck their breath in when they realise that the smooth tenure of the service is to be hijacked by a baptism. They sigh to each other, 'Well we've got to remember they are the future church,' which makes Tom grit his teeth and say, 'Correction, they're our present church.'

Audrey

Monday 28th May

Dear God,

It's Tom's birthday today. He's wearing much better than I am, and that's without any moisturiser, night cream and Loving Care no.70 that covers all grey. Maybe it's the Sugar Puffs.

I gave him *St Augustine's Confessions*. Anthony and Martin each gave him a poster for his study, one of flowers saying, 'Blossom where you are', and the other of two wheeling seagulls saying, 'They can because they think they can'. Derek bought him a paperweight embossed with praying hands. So that's the SPCK shop cleared out.

Audrey

Thursday 31st May
The Visit of the Blessed Virgin Mary to Elizabeth

Dear God,

I don't know what came over me tonight. Had Father Benton around for dinner this evening. He asked me what I missed most about my former life and in an unguarded moment I said, 'Money! Money! Money!'

'Of course you do,' he said. Oh God, what a relief to be honest, but then one always can with clergy. They've been there too.

You know we have to budget so tightly that under the column 'Riotous Living' come door to door collections, birthday presents and haircuts. The nearest we ever get to decadence are the beef sandwiches with horse-radish sauce and a half pint of bitter shandy we indulge in on a Monday.

Please God, stop the budget I want to get off!

Audrey

Sunday 3rd June
Pentecost (Whit Sunday)

Dear God,

Doris Stubbs has done her nut in St Jude's. She's been carried away by Pentecostal fire and created a massive arrangement of branches, driftwood, cones and seed-pods and sprayed the whole lot with the remains of a red aerosol left over from Christmas.

The choir couldn't see the congregation, the congregation couldn't see the choir, and neither could see Tom as she'd chosen the pulpit as the centre of the conflagration.

Audrey

Tuesday 5th June
Tuesday in Whitsun Week.
Boniface, Bishop, Missionary Martyr, 754

Dear God,
   Tom's sent Doris Stubbs a note of thanks for the forest
fire on Sunday and has begged her to let him know when it
all gets too much for her.

Audrey

Wednesday 6th June
Ember Day

Dear God,
   Doris Stubbs called this morning to assure Tom that she had many flower-arranging years in her yet. Said she had some good ideas for next Harvest Festival, but that she was keeping them under wraps for the moment. Tom thought that a good idea.

Audrey

PS   Mother says Tom is frightened of Doris Stubbs. I think she's right.

Thursday 7th June

Dear God,
   Maybe you do have a little joke sometimes, but why liturgical dance? I get quite unnerved when figures suddenly materialise on the chancel steps stretching and swaying, weaving and ducking. I lose track of the theme and forget the message watching the goose-pimpled legs and deciding that Madge Kemp and Doris Smith, who are the wrong side of fifty, must be on hormone replacement therapy.
   Did you know God that fifty percent of parishioners are called Doris and the other fifty percent Madge?

Audrey

Friday 8th June
Ember Day

Dear God,
    Peeped into Tom's diary this morning:

9am	See the burglar alarm people.
10.30am	Check the church thermostat.
12.15pm	Meet the churchwardens and painters re church hall redecoration. Discuss colour schemes.
2–4pm	Meeting with magazine production team.
8pm	Deanery meeting re parish quota.

At his induction the bishop said, 'Tom, above all be a loving and praying presence in their midst. Bring them the love of God and don't worry about anything else'. But it's so difficult when one's day is filled with burglar alarms, thermostats, finances and colour charts, and when 'harvest beige' and 'honeysuckle yellow' are the last words he remembers when he goes to sleep.

Audrey

Saturday 9th June
Ember Day.
Columba, Abbot of Iona, Missionary, 597

Dear God,
    Today I went to a dream wedding; the wedding of Susan Mary and James, two young people we have come to know very well and of whom we are so fond.
    'Wouldn't every girl want to look like that on her wedding day,' whispered a young woman behind me as Susan came down the aisle.
    The flowers, the music, the hymns, chosen with such care

and thought by them both, were matched by Tom's words right from his heart to them.

'It is God who has brought you to this church to marry one another. It is he who has united perfectly your souls. It is he who has blessed you and sends you out into the community as husband and wife. But no man and no woman has in themselves unlimited love. The love you have will dry up unless you draw upon the limitless love of God. Love cannot be sustained without God. It's not love that sustains marriage, it's marriage that sustains love, and the will to make it work comes from God.

'And so James and Susan, in a moment or two we will go to the high altar where you will kneel in the presence of God. There prayers will be said for you and then, together with all your friends and family, you will again receive God's blessing.

'As you leave this house of God this afternoon remember he loves you both in a manner so complete and perfect that you will never completely understand it in this life. Because of this love he has for you and because of what he has done for you, if you bring to him in your marriage all your joys, difficulties and sorrows, I know your marriage will be as long as you both shall live.'

God, I thought it was only the mother of the bride who was supposed to cry.

Audrey

Sunday 10th June
Trinity Sunday
Pentecost 1 (Trinity Sunday)

Dear God,
    Today we celebrated the Holy Trinity: God the Father, God the Son and God the Holy Spirit—the three in one. It's hard to comprehend God and harder still to explain. Or is it?

Here I am sharing with you my hopes and fears, and the ups and downs of my life and family, because I know you love and care for me.

Each Sunday I receive the body and blood of your Son, Jesus Christ, with the words, 'The body of Christ keep you in eternal life' and 'The blood of Christ keep you in eternal life.' Every day I witness the action of the Holy Spirit in people's lives as they love, care and forgive each other.

If I were asked what the ultimate reality is that underpins my life, I would have to say like St Paul: 'The grace of the Lord Jesus Christ and the love of God and the fellowship of the Holy Spirit'.

Audrey

Monday 11th June
St Barnabas the Apostle

Dear God,

Had a day out in London today. Went into All Souls, Langham Place before lunch to sit quietly and to take the weight off our feet.

We weren't the only ones. At least a dozen or so business-men and women came in to sit and pray. This action of the Holy Spirit that brings them from their high tech offices and shops was humbling to observe, and I've had to rearrange my ideas of the big bad world out there. You just can't tell, can you God?

We then moved on to St James' Park to eat our sand-wiches, lying on the grass in the warm sun with the rest of London.

Later, we made for Harrods to window shop and to buy a quarter of their handmade chocolates which we consumed on the train coming home.

Audrey

Tuesday 12th June

Dear God,
   Philippa phoned this evening–just to unload and have a cry on my shoulder. Said she had to talk to someone who'd got it together, knew where they were going and what it was all about!
   It seems that her boss/boy friend of three years standing is not going to leave his wife (who doesn't understand him) after all.
   Oh God, I feel such a fraud. You know just how confused I am most of the time, but she was depending on me. I asked myself if I should tell her that when I'm hurt, angry or sad I just go and sit in the empty church and, keeping my eyes on the cross, visualise myself walking hand in hand with the person concerned up to that cross? Should I tell her that I visualise myself unloading all the anger, sadness and hurt that burdens me at the foot of the cross, prayerfully leaving it there for your healing?
   Well, I did just that and then held my breath for an adverse reaction or, worse, a flippant remark. After a while she said, 'Maybe I was meant to phone you.'
   God, help all the Philippas of this world who'd be surprised if they knew just how much they give to people like me.

Audrey

Thursday 14th June
Fathers of the Eastern Church. Basil the Great, Bishop of Caesarea, Teacher of the Faith, 379
Thanksgiving for the Institution of Holy Communion. *Corpus Christi*

Dear God,
   Something's gone wrong with our bi-monthly Christian

Aid Hunger Lunches. Soup, brown bread, cheese and coffee is what's on offer, but Mr Barnes has started bringing his own supply of butter because he says at his age things won't go down.

Today, Miss Flowers sneaked in two pieces of honey roasted ham and a tomato in a Tupperware box, and Doreen Brown handed round a box of after dinner mints she'd been given with the coffee.

Tom says not to worry even if they wheel in the sweets trolley, as long as we get the money.

Audrey

Friday 15th June

Dear God,

Please help me to remember that a quick word with Constance Prescott is not to be had and that I must never ring her in prime time. This morning I was treated to a half hour run through of the voluntary organisations she runs and how her friends say, 'Which hat are you wearing today, Con?'

Audrey

Saturday 16th June

Dear God,

'Caritas' is what they called the pilgrimage of four to five thousand Christians to the Ardingly showgrounds today. 'Caritas' means 'love' and love is what overwhelmed us all at this day of renewal, rekindling and encouragement.

We were all there, evangelicals, charismatics and anglo-

Catholics, for a day of preparation and prayer as we stand on the threshold of the Decade of Evangelism.

I can't recreate the atmosphere of the day on paper, but then I don't need to, for you were there in the prayers, in the singing, in the testimonies and in the addresses by Bishop John Taylor this morning, and Bishop Michael Marshall this afternoon.

You were there in the fun that Roger Royle lent the day as compere. You were there in the sheer joy of thousands of people sharing their common faith together. You were there on their faces and in their hearts as they climbed into their cars and coaches at 5 o'clock and went home.

Bishop Taylor defined evangelism as, 'The process, by whatever means, that brings a person from not believing into a saving faith in Jesus Christ.' He read St John chapter 3 verse 16, 'For God so loved the world that he gave his only Son, that whoever believes in him should not perish but have eternal life'.

He said that the five propositions here were that God loves us, that Jesus Christ died for us, that we have got something to be saved from, that there is judgment and that we are all accountable and must put our trust in Jesus Christ and find life, all wrapped up in that magnificent gospel text.

'Those five propositions,' he said 'have to be translated into language that people who read *The Sun* and the *Daily Mirror* can understand, as well as the handful of people who read *The Times*, *The Independent* and *The Telegraph*. That is the challenge before us—to translate those five gospel truths into language everyone can understand.

'How else can they be helped to know that they are loved, that someone died for them, that they are at risk, that they are accountable and that they can find faith and life in Jesus Christ?'

Finally, he read from St Matthew's Gospel chapter 28, verse 18,

And Jesus came and said to them, 'All authority in heaven and on earth has been given to me. Go therefore and make disciples of all nations, baptizing them in the name of the Father and of the Son and of the Holy Spirit, teaching them to observe all that I have commanded you; and lo, I am with you always, to the close of the age'.

He left us with this final thought: 'What if, at the end of the Decade of Evangelism, as the year 2000 strikes, everything stops because Christ comes back, because the world blows sky high, or because some ghastly terror disease strikes the whole human race? What if it all ends in the year 2000? How would you use these coming ten years if you knew that? Do that and you'll obey Christ's command.'

From the biggest marquee I've ever been in came the sound of thousands of voices singing the hymn 'Take my life, and let it be'.

By lunchtime Miss Flowers, who'd feared it would all be too happy clappy, enthusiastic and undignified, began to relax. Seeing our bishop set the final seal of approval on the day for her, and she even ventured that it was a pity more of St Jude's people hadn't come.

After we'd eaten our packed lunches, relaxing in the sun around the grounds, we went back for the afternoon session and an address from Bishop Michael Marshall.

'Christianity is not another philosophy, Christianity is not another ideology, Christianity is not any "thing". Christianity is "somebody",' he said. 'It is Jesus–Jesus and the resurrection. It is Jesus the body of Christ.'

He said, 'I have a few secret fears about the Decade of Evangelism. I love our church, but isn't it marvellous, we've called for a Decade of Evangelism but it mustn't start till January the 6th next year. We mustn't get too carried away; it's got to stop by the year 2000!'

He pointed out that we don't talk about witnessing in Anglicanism. 'We leave our Baptist friends to convert them and then, if they graduate, we invite them to the Anglican Church.'

'My friends,' he said, 'I want to witness today. I'm an

evangelical, I've experienced the real presence of Jesus through the Scriptures. I'm a Catholic because I've experienced the real presence of Jesus in the blessed sacrament to which the only response is adoration and worship. But, I'm a charismatic as well, for I've experienced his healing power in my life and through my ministry. What did the bishop say to me when he ordained me? "Receive the Holy Spirit for the work and office of a priest". Renewal is for the whole church. Generally the church was most in a mess when it was being renewed.

'I believe that deep in the subconscious of at least the Western world there is still the face of Jesus,' he said, 'and the only place they are going to see the face of Jesus is in the face of the church.'

He invited us to stand and take hold of a piece of the body of Christ next to us, that hand in hand we might indeed pray a prayer of rededication, renewal and refreshment.

Holy Communion followed with the body and blood of Christ being administered from many points in the marquee to thousands of Anglicans of many traditions.

The last hymn was, of course, 'Shine Jesus Shine' and Miss Flowers, St Jude's member on the Deanery Synod, was swaying and raising her arms. The Rector of St Jude's was clapping and swaying, and the wife of the Rector of St Jude's was doing the same and was quite carried away.

St Jude's seemed far away.

Oh God, I'm still on a high. I feel I've glimpsed what could be. I know I'm going on a bit, but for me and for Tom and I'm sure for Miss Flowers too, today will always burn like a bright light.

Audrey

Sunday 17th June
Second Sunday after Pentecost
Theme: The Church's Unity and Fellowship

Dear God,

Miss Flowers is in love with Tom. She hangs on his every word and told me this morning that she thought he was a 'lovely man'. Is she another 'curate's peril'? Should I worry about her?

I would have agreed with her yesterday God, but not today. Yesterday he fixed the dripping tap in the bathroom and said he liked my new hair colour. Today he left shaving cream all over the mirror and his unlovely whiskers in the wash basin.

I told Philippa about the 'lovely man' bit when she phoned tonight. Said she'd never met a 'lovely man' yet. She's still feeling very fragile.

It's his smile that does it God. He's got good teeth. Got them from his grandfather who was always introduced as 'This is grandfather, he's ninety-two with all his own teeth.'

But to get back to Miss Flowers, as the course of true love never runs straight, I'm sure the scales will soon fall from her eyes.

Maybe I should have her over here to witness the goings on when her 'lovely man' finds out that his youngest son, who's been making his own windsurfing board, has left his father's Black and Decker work bench stuck up with a mixture of resin and fibreglass. And he will soon God!

Audrey

Wednesday 20th June
Translation of Edward, King of West Saxons

Dear God,

If houses go to heaven, Lavender Cottage, 2 Spring Lane,

complete with its own her Polly Nightingale and her wheel-chair will. I can see them now ascending through the clouds.

When I'm feeling swamped by it all I drop in on Polly. When Tom's feeling ragged and people-pressured he drops in on Polly. Through her gentleness and quiet sense of humour she ministers to us, never expecting us to be other than ourselves.

She hasn't much of this world's goods, but as I step through her door I feel I've stepped into an ante-room of heaven and I come away lifted and refreshed.

Audrey

Saturday 23rd June

Dear God,
   Today at 2.30pm there were 'Cream Teas in the Rectory Garden. Entrance Fee £1.'

By 8.30am the Mothers' Union had manned the rectory kitchen and Tom had retreated to his study to eat his Sugar Puffs. Martin had gone back to bed.

11.30am found wall to wall scones cooling on every flat surface and Tom with his head round the kitchen door saying, 'Marvellous ladies, marvellous. Keep up the good work. What would St Jude's do without you?'

At 12 o'clock the Men's Society dragged tables and chairs over from the hall and the rain arrived with the first guests at 2.30pm.

There followed a general invasion of the rectory, with the overflow from the dining-room, lounge, study and kitchen settling down with their cups of tea and cream scones on the stairs.

Mother busied herself down on her hands and knees between the varicose veins and walking sticks, wiping up blobs of cream and jam and pools of tea.

It was all over by 5 o'clock and so was the rain. Mother got off her knees and then fished out the bits of cream scones down the sides of the chairs. Martin came out of his bedroom and the cat came down from the roof. We made £67.

Audrey

Sunday 24th June
Third Sunday after Pentecost.
Theme: The Birth of St John the Baptist

Dear God,

St Jude's really makes me cringe sometimes. There's no slipping into church unnoticed on a Sunday for a quiet hour with you.

If you're a newcomer you're weighed up by the church-wardens, sidesmen, Madge Dunbar and Doris Stubbs, all with a hidden agenda behind their welcoming smiles. (a) Are you just passing trade or do you live in the parish? (b) If the latter, have you any organisational skills, 'cause we need people for the youth club? (c) Can you add up a shopping list, because we're looking for a treasurer? (d) Have you ever sung a note in tune, because the choir's getting a bit thin? (e) Have you anything tucked away in your background: a title, a DSO, an OBE or the like, because we need someone of substance to lead our fund-raising team? (f) If you're a woman, let's fill up your diary and blow your mind for the next year with cream teas, jumble sales, flower-arranging, magazine distribution, church cleaning, spring fairs, summer fairs, autumn and Christmas fairs.

If they don't find out at the door as you come in, they'll find out over a cup of coffee in the hall afterwards.

A Mr and Mrs Roberts arrived for the Eucharist this morning. Afterwards at coffee, Major Crabtree and Madge Dunbar, in two quick moves, separated their quarry. Major Crabtree had Mr Roberts in one corner ascertaining that he was indeed an accountant, while Madge Dunbar, backed up by Miss Willis and Doris Stubbs, had Mrs Roberts in another corner inferring that the way to heaven was through flower-arranging, jumble sales and cream teas.

God, Mr and Mrs Roberts came to St Jude's this morning seeking spiritual refreshment! With their working week probably filled with the school run, homework, deadlines, targets and profit margins, and their Saturdays spent mending bicycles, mowing lawns and taking children to swings and bouncy castles, they should not be pounced on, sized up, and their lives further reorganised by St Jude's.

Must get Tom to have a word with the PCC, because I'm not sure we'll see Mr Roberts again. As for Mrs Roberts, from the hunted look on her face I saw this morning, she's probably not stopped running yet.

Audrey

Monday 25th June

Dear God,

Yes, we're having a Flower Festival at St Jude's. We're taking as our theme 'Fruits of the Spirit', and I'm doing 'joy'. It's sent us all back to our Bibles to that wonderful passage in Galatians, chapter 5, verse 22. Quite a challenge translating love, joy, peace, patience, kindness, goodness, faithfulness, gentleness and self-control into flowers. We have a month to think about it.

I'm sure you'll like whatever I do God, but will Doris Stubbs? She's in overall charge, of course, and has already called a meeting of the Flower Festival Flower-Arrangers.

During the festival there'll be cream teas in the hall. The Mothers' Union has undertaken to organise this and has formed the Flower Festival Cream Tea Catering Committee.

Music is to be played at regular intervals on the organ by Mr Taylor and liturgical dance will be performed at 11am and 3.30pm each day. Alice Kemp is in charge here, with the first meeting of the Flower Festival Liturgical Dance Group taking place tonight.

I think I'll design my display on paper first. This will be the last time the flowers stay where I put them. I don't mind if mine's not the best, but please don't let it be the worst!

Audrey

Tuesday 26th June

Dear God,

Today is the anniversary of Tom's ordination. At Holy Communion this morning he gave thanks for his ministry and we prayed for all those to be ordained this year at Petertide. My mind went back to that great turning point in our lives— the culmination of so much prayer, resulting in so many changes.

Tom, Martin, Mother and I went for a steak at the Dog and Duck to mark the occasion. After a second glass of champagne Mother said she'd never thought he'd stick it this long. Martin, after two Cokes, said he thought his Dad's sermons had improved.

Took ages to get to sleep last night God. I had carnations, daisies, vases, bits of florist's wire and Doris Stubbs all bunching together in my mind. At about 2am I settled on a sunburst of deep yellows to express 'joy'. At about 3am I'd wired every bloom with florist's wire and positioned them in a mountain of oasis. Then I went to sleep.

Audrey

Wednesday 27th June
Ember Day

Dear God,

Here are a rector's four four letter words: LORD, PRAY, HYMN, SAVE.

Here are the wife of the rector's four four letter words: TEAS, BAKE, WORK, HELP!

Audrey

Thursday 28th June
Irenaeus, Bishop of Lyons, Martyr, c 200

Dear God,

Three cheers for Tom's godfather who died last month and left Tom £926. Of course Tom straightaway reached for our folder of unpaid accounts, but I reminded him of his sermon only last Sunday, when he preached so enthusiastically on having 'life abundant' and reckoned that a holiday in France would be abundant enough for me. He's going to sleep on it.

Tom always sleeps on things, God. I'm sure that when you say, 'Come thou good and faithful servant,' he'll say, 'Thank you God, I'll just sleep on it.'

Audrey

Friday 29th June
St Peter the Apostle. Ember Day

Dear God,

We're going to France! I can't believe it! I thought I'd

never get Tom out of England. Bye bye *Angleterre, Allez Dordogne*!

We're going on the overnight ferry from Portsmouth to Le Havre and driving down to the Dordogne – all on the wrong side of the road!

Please God, breathe new life into Josephine; she's suffering from a terminal case of rust. Tom administered the last rites this morning when she wouldn't start and nearly broke his foot.

Audrey

Saturday 30th June
Ember Day

Dear God,

Mother popped round this evening to remind us that we haven't seen all of England yet and left a pamphlet on 'Historic Hastings'.

Ninety percent of the cathedral clergy holiday in France. You know when they've been there because their sermons are peppered with French phrases. It's all so impressive. God, I'm going to learn French.

Audrey

Sunday 1st July
Fourth Sunday after Pentecost
Theme: The Church's Mission to the Individual

Dear God,

At the Eucharist this morning we prayed again for those to be ordained this Petertide, for their families, for the parishes where they will serve, and for their theological colleges.

Tom recalled his own ordination. He described the silent retreat taken by him and the other ordinands immediately before their ordination, with the extraordinary atmosphere of tension and spirituality. 'One comes away from the ordination service with a feeling of indescribable grace perhaps known only to those who have been ordained,' he said.

He reminded us that we are called to pray for those to be ordained during the Ember days in Advent, Lent, Petertide and Michaelmas. Cranmer was right, he said, to include in the Book of Common Prayer a prayer to be said at every Holy Communion service:

> 'Give grace, O heavenly Father, to all Bishops and Curates, that they may both by their life and doctrine set forth thy true and lively Word, and rightly and duly administer thy holy Sacraments.'

Had one of the Miss Pattersons on the phone this evening very upset. Said she'd witnessed something that in all her church going years she'd never seen before and hoped she'd never see again. She'd seen, she said, Mr Taylor our organist shaking his fist at one of the choir during the Gloria this morning.

Tom thanked her for her call and said he'd have a word with Mr Taylor and see what it was all about.

Audrey

Monday 2nd July
Visitation of the Blessed Virgin Mary

Dear God,
The rectory looks as if we're about to have another jumble sale. Anthony arrived home yesterday with every

single possession he owns and those he doesn't. Evidently at the end of the academic year the students have to literally 'clear out'.

It's nice to have my toasted sandwich-maker back, and it's good to know where my favourite coffee mug got to. We've also solved the mystery of Tom's missing belt.

Derek's home too, but not for long as he's landed a summer job at Butlins. I tried to persuade Anthony that he might like to join him, but he says he couldn't be parted from Julie, Karen, Tina and Leigh Ann for that long, and anyway he's been invited to spend two weeks on Leigh Ann's daddy's gin palace moored in the Solent.

Do you know God that most of the clothes Anthony wears have been given to him by his adoring fans? The blue sweater to match his eyes was from Tina. The latest T shirt to show off his tanned muscles was given by Julie, and the new Levi jeans were bought by Miranda—and her father an archdeacon! What's the matter with these girls God?

Audrey

Tuesday 3rd July
St Thomas the Apostle

Dear God,

Martin has resurrected his French primer and tells me it's a doddle. Miss Ashworth has lent me *French Made Easy*. Mr Vern has brought round his set of tapes *French is Fun*, and Madge Dunbar has given me half a tube of insect repellent. Forgive my vanity, but I've always wanted a GB sticker.

Audrey

PS Why *did* Martin fail French if it's such a doddle?

Wednesday 4th July
Translation of St Martin, Bishop and Confessor

Dear God,

Met Debbie at a clergy wives' 'get together' this morning. She told me that Father Gary has done ten weddings, fourteen baptisms and thirteen funerals since his induction. He just presses two keys on his Amstrad and, hey presto, there are his records.

She told me that Father Gary has a fax machine too. Who does he fax—the Archbishop of Canterbury, the Pope, or you God?

Of course they have an answering machine. Debbie says she's not going to be an unpaid telephonist. I can see them now at the end of the day sorting out all the calls in descending order of importance.

I just have to answer the phone in case it's Littlewoods!

Apparently Father Gary also has a surgery every Thursday afternoon between 2.30 and 4.30 when parishioners can come and cry on his shoulder (by appointment of course).

It makes Tom's ministry seem quite haphazard, happening as it so often does in the street, in the supermarket between the beans and the sweetcorn, in the post office, or on the phone at 11 o'clock at night.

Please help me God. I'm beginning to dislike Father Gary and I don't even really know him. It's just that we don't seem to be able to organise St Jude's congregation like that. They feel that Tom is there for them whenever and wherever they need him. I suppose you are too God.

Audrey

PS   This time next month we'll be on our way to France. Roll on the fourth of August!

Thursday 5th July

Oh God,

When you're seventeen your friends don't die; they wear Doc Marten's, they windsurf, they don't get up in the morning, they play 'Tie Your Mother Down', but God they don't die.

At seventeen you're immortal. Death happens to other people, not to your friends. But Dale died today and all the great medical advances could not save him.

Martin went straight to his room when he came back from college with the news. I wanted to comfort him, tell him that it was your will, that the friend he'd laughed and joked with is now in a better place and that it was all for the best. But what could I say in the face of something so seemingly senseless to him, and to me?

Tom says we cannot take away the hurt, he has to go through it himself and we must just be there for him with our love and our prayers.

Oh God, is it all right to be angry with you?

Audrey

Friday 6th July
Thomas More, Martyr, 1535

Dear God,

Tom has just come home from choir practice having spoken to Mr Taylor. He'd been moved to shake his fist last Sunday because one of the Barber mafia, who's just come up to the choir from Sunday school, started to open and hand around a packet of crisps as the first note of the Gloria was struck.

Evidently it had the desired effect, as I suppose having a fist shaken at one in church would, and the culprit shrank back into the dark wood of the choir stalls and misericords, taking his smokey bacon crisps with him.

Audrey

Saturday 7th July

Dear God,
   Ran into Debbie in Woolworth's this afternoon. Said she'd left Father Gary at home gnashing his teeth.
   Their tabby, Pussykins, who'd been curled up at his feet while he was putting the finishing touches to tomorrow's sermon, had suddenly spied a woodlouse. Galvanised into action, he'd pursued his prey under the desk. With a final pounce he'd dragged the computer plug from its socket, leaving Father Gary staring at a blank screen. Gone was his sermon to St Bede's he'd been agonising over all morning. Gone was Pussykins, sent into orbit. He was going to have to write it all again tonight and miss *Blind Date*.
   Tom is still chuckling to himself.

Audrey

Sunday 8th July
Fifth Sunday after Pentecost
Theme: The Church's Mission to All Men

Dear God,
   Today is Sea Sunday. The introit hymn was 'Oh God, our help in ages past' and the offertory hymn 'Eternal Father, strong to save', both popular with the older men who reminisced at coffee about their navy days.
   The Sunday school had made a frieze depicting Jesus calming the storm, which they unrolled across the chancel

steps – all ten feet of it. Granted some of the disciples were wearing trainers and the boat depicted looked more like the winner of the Whitbread Round the World Race, but it was a magnificent effort.

Wally Burt led the intercessory prayers again. What would he do with Sea Sunday, I wondered?

(1) We pray for all those who brave the storms of life.

(2) We pray for all who founder on the rocks of distress, loneliness and bereavement.

(3) We pray for those drowning in a sea of pain. Help them to know that when the waves of life break over them you are there.

(4) Lead us to steer the right course, to keep our eyes on the only horizon, so that we may come safely into the harbour. (I think he was a bit confused here, because if you kept your eyes on the horizon you'd sail straight out to sea again!)

(5) And we remember those for whom the sands of life have run out and who are now at anchor.

By now I felt thoroughly wet and seasick.

Audrey

Tuesday 10th July

Dear God,

Inconspicuous service for the church is no longer possible. The vote was carried at the last PCC that the office bearers at St Jude's be photographed and displayed on a large board in the church porch. This has now been done and we're all smiling brightly as if we've got the 'whole world in our hands'.

I didn't recognise some of them. I've never seen Wally Burt smile before and Doris Stubbs had had a mahogany rinse for the occasion.

They do this at the supermarkets – the current managers etc – not that they're ever around when, for some deeply profound reason, the gravy powder's been moved, or you want to tell them they'll go to hell alive for opening on Sundays.

Anyway, it seems that the church has to be marketed too. It all comes under the umbrella called 'communication'.

It was also decided that Tom and I should be photographed with Sally and Pooky to make us 'more accessible'. I still bear the scratch marks.

But God we end up knowing a lot about everybody else, not much about ourselves, and the only person we really want to see is the managing director–you.

Audrey

Friday 13th July

Dear God,

St Jude's has been 'done' again. They came back for what they couldn't carry last time: two silver vases, the chancel carpet and the 'Retired Donkey's of Cairo' collection box. There's not much left to take now except the pulpit, the lectern and the rector.

Audrey

Saturday 14th July

Dear God,

Had a mammoth cleaning up of the church grounds today because the archdeacon's coming round for his inspection next Thursday. There was much weeding, lopping, cutting, mowing and raking up of several years growth.

At one point Mrs Burt came to Tom in a high state of excitement saying she'd found the Longbottom twins under a thick layer of leaf mould in the furthest recesses of the churchyard. Tom said she should get them out quickly before their mother had a fit. She replied rather icily that, as they'd been there since 1832, she felt they should stay put.

By mid morning the weather had warmed up considerably and the rector was down to shorts only. The sight of so much holy, hairy flesh, muscle and sweat was too much for the Misses Patterson who, mumbling something about a prior engagement, left, missing a fine spread put on by the Mothers' Union in the hall for the workers after the last leaf had been raked up.

I'm sure that at the end of the world, there will be cups of tea, iced fairy cakes, sandwiches and cold sausage rolls that stick to the roof of your mouth, put on by the Mothers' Union for all who make it through the pearly gates. I hope there's a good slug of brandy for those who don't.

Audrey

PS   I dreamed last night that as I passed through the pearly gates the Mothers' Union were raffling a knitted St Peter.

Sunday 15th July
Sixth Sunday after Pentecost
Theme: The New Man

Dear God,
Why is it that the Eucharist on a Sunday is more deeply satisfying sometimes than at other times? It was like that for me this morning. It wasn't any special Sunday–no processions, no special floral decorations, no earth moving sermon (sorry Tom), just the usual faces and number of communicants, but as we moved slowly up to the communion rail and the choir softly sang

> 'Soul of my Saviour, sanctify my breast,
> Body of Christ, be thou my saving guest,
> Blood of my Saviour, bathe me in thy tide,
> Wash me with water flowing from thy side'.

a feeling of deep peace, almost invulnerability, swept over me.

Time and again people say to me or to Tom, 'You know, I didn't feel like coming to church this morning but I'm so glad I did.' Maybe it's the same for them too God.

Maybe it's all in direct proportion to what we put into a service, coming as participants and not as spectators.

Audrey

Tuesday 17th July

Dear God,

Met Debbie at the library. Says that Father Gary has now lost his whole parish, just like that, 'in the twinkling of an eye,' and that he's been up since 6am sitting in front of his Amstrad 9512 looking for them.

Tom's been wearing a silly grin and humming around the rectory all day.

Audrey

PS   Mr James rang this evening to say that Anne was taken into the hospice this afternoon. Oh God, just be there for them both.

Wednesday 18th July

Dear God,
   At the fair on Saturday we're running a Men's Lib Cake Competition.

St Jude's Mens' Lib Cake Competition

Conditions of Entry

No female assistance whatsoever is permissible. The ingredients shown below must be used. Entries should be brought to St Jude's hall on Friday between 7pm–9pm. Entries will be available for sale at the cake stall after judging on Saturday 21st July. The certificate overleaf should be completed and accompany each entry.

Recipe

8 oz self raising flour	2 eggs
5 oz margarine	8 oz mixed fruit
5 oz castor sugar	

Oven gas 3, 335 F, 170 C

Method

1) Grease and line a 7 inch cake tin with grease proof paper.
2) Cream the margarine and sugar in a mixing bowl until light and fluffy.
3) Beat in the eggs one at a time, adding a little of the sieved flour with the second.
4) Fold in half the remaining flour and fruit gently and thoroughly until well mixed.
5) Fold in half the milk.
6) Repeat with the remainder of the dry ingredients and finally fold in the remaining milk.
7) Put in cake tin and smooth the top.
8) Bake in a preheated oven for 1 3/4–2 hours.
9) Test the cake before removing by inserting a warmed skewer (or knitting needle) which should come out clean when the cake is ready.

Audrey

Thursday 19th July

Dear God,

Tom made his cake tonight. After carefully measuring out the ingredients with the precision of a scientist he ignored instructions 2 to 6, threw them all into the mixer, turned it on to maximum speed and sat down to have a good read of the newspaper. Fifteen minutes later he scraped the mixture into the cake tin and popped it into the oven, declaring that he didn't know what all the fuss and mystery was about baking.

The first bit of the mystery appeared when the outside was golden brown, but the inside, revealed with the jab of a knitting needle, was still raw. The mystery deepened further when ten minutes later the outside was very well done and the middle still uncooked.

Finally, the knitting needle came out clean. The tin was removed from the oven, and turned upside down. A rather burnt, lopsided disc fell onto the cake rack, at which point Tom raised his eyes to heaven and said, 'Oh Audrey, the things I do for Jesus.'

I hurried him to sign the certificate. Heaven forbid that anyone should think I was implicated in that.

Certificate

I certify that this cake is the result of my own unaided effort, that there has been no female participation of any sort and that only the ingredients specified have been used.

Signed *Tom Carter*

Date *19th July.*

Audrey

Friday 20th July
Margaret, Virgin and Martyr at Antioch

Dear God,

Stall holders and helpers gathered in the hall this evening to position the trestle tables and to sort out who's helping where at the fair tomorrow.

Mrs Burt says that she and her brother Mr Venn have been on jams and pickles at St Jude's Summer Fair since they were children and they're not changing now.

The Barber family say they have had the trestle table below the stage for the cakes since the war and they're not changing now.

I say we should each put £10 into a kitty and forget about the whole thing. I've made so much fudge I feel crystallised. I think I'll stay in bed tomorrow till it's all over.

Mrs Prestcott brought around two banana loaves this morning. Made me promise they wouldn't be sold for a penny less than £2 each, otherwise it would be a waste of her time and ingredients. I shall have to keep them away from Nellie Barber who sells everything for 50p.

Had a phone call from Philippa tonight. Says she's coming down for the fair and could she help?! Oh God, the Philippa's of this world don't help they just decorate. Well, I'll let her loose with my fudge and see if she can shift that.

Audrey

Saturday 21st July

Dear God,

I can't believe it, the Summer Fair made £739.26p. Quite amazing when you think that most of the stalls were stocked with recycled rubbish and things that have been at the back of cupboards and drawers for years.

There was some rivalry between cakes and jams and pickles, but Miss Flowers soon defused the tension by reminding them that we were all working for your glory God and not for the glory of cakes, jams and pickles. She really comes up trumps sometimes.

The raffle table did a brisk trade. There were two bottles of claret to be won and a large Spanish doll to hide one's nightdress, crocheted by the Misses Patterson.

When Philippa arrived in her ridiculously high heels, looking as though she'd stepped right out of a Harrods window, I gave her the job of hawking the tray of fudge I'd made around the hall. She did a wonderful job, making for the men first of course. First she urged them to buy it for their wives and grandchildren. Then she urged them to buy it for their girlfriends and typists. Finally she urged them to buy it because it had been made by the holy hands of the rector's wife, who was watching them across the hall. What really helped was the promotional blurb she'd pinned across her chest which read, 'Naughty but Nice'.

I tried to disown her, but I needn't have worried; she was a great hit and had sold the lot in the first hour.

A special table was set aside for the Men's Lib Competition Cakes. By 10.30am judging was underway by Miss Wentworth from the home economics department of the local comprehensive. There were twenty-nine entries in all with only one worse than Tom's and that was Wally Burt's. He'd taken an even shorter cut than Tom and used the microwave.

Miss Wentworth cut a small wedge from each one, examining the texture and having a little taste. When she came to entries twenty-eight and twenty-nine, Tom's and Wally's respectively, she abandoned the tasting bit.

Cecil Dunbar won the prize for the best cake, which pleased Madge no end, and why not, it had her hand prints all over it, even down to the silver doily and the silver tray.

The cakes then went on sale, and in a rush of compassion and blood to the head, I bought Tom's and Wally's. One I smothered with custard for dinner, and the other I gave to Sally who thought Christmas had arrived early, but I won't tell which!

Audrey

Sunday 22nd July
Seventh Sunday after Pentecost
Theme: St Mary Magdalene

Dear God,

I inherited Christianity. I was baptised, I was sent to Sunday school and I sang 'Onward! Christian soldiers' while the boys threw hassocks at each other.

At fourteen I was confirmed. I wore a white dress, a white veil and the little gold cross my parents had given me to mark the occasion.

I don't remember any of the preparation for confirmation except for one thing the priest said to us at the end, 'Remember, there are strong Christians, there are weak Christians and there are middling Christians and God loves them equally.'

Even today those words rebuke me when I'm being critical of fellow Christians, and comfort me when I fall short.

What a hotchpotch we make together at St Jude's: Doris Stubbs, Madge Dunbar, myself, Polly Nightingale, Wally Burt, Mrs Venn, Major Crabtree, Primrose Flowers and Harry our alcoholic gardener.

What an unholy mix of personalities, strengths and weaknesses come to the communion rail to share together the body and blood of Jesus Christ and to realise the words we have just heard:

We are the Body of Christ.
In the one Spirit we were all baptised into one body.

Let us then pursue all that makes for peace and builds up our common life.

Audrey

Monday 23rd July

Dear God,

If Tom is to have any sort of a day off I have to assume the role of a guard dog on a Monday to keep the St Jude's flock at bay. Please forgive me for the following white lies I've told so far today when the phone has rung: At 8.17am I said he was not with us when he was asleep; at 8.48am I said he was out when he was paying the milkman on the drive; at 9.25am I said he was not available when he was shaving; at 9.47am I said he was otherwise engaged when he was playing with Sally on the lawn; at 10.05am I said they'd just missed him when he'd bolted to the loo on the first ring of the telephone; at 4.35pm I bit off that nice undertaker's head when he said it was all right for some.

I've lined them all up to phone Tom at 9 o'clock tomorrow morning, but now he tells me he's arranged to see the bishop. Perhaps the bishop would like to see me too 'cause I'm not hanging around here at that time!

Audrey

Tuesday 24th July

Dear God,

An urgent prayer for Josephine tonight who goes for her MOT (moment of truth) at 11.30am tomorrow. I know Tom is worried about her failing and the expense that will ensue.

I know she looks awful, but I've vacuumed out all Sally's

hairs, cleaned out all the sweet wrappers on my side, and put a St Christopher medal on the dashboard. Oh God, she's got to be all right, we're going to France next week, remember?

Tom says that as long as they don't open the bonnet, look underneath, try to open the boot, test the clutch, the brakes, the rear lights, or look at the speedometer, she should pass. He says there are more dicey things under her bonnet than this world dreams of.

I suppose there will be some expense, but please let it be small.

Audrey

Wednesday 25th July
St James the Apostle

Dear God,
Praise be! Josephine's passed. Now you'd have thought Tom would have jumped for joy. Instead, he went quite pale when the garage rang to say she'd passed and said, 'It makes me sweat to think of all the lethal heaps of scrap metal that are allowed on our roads!'

Audrey

Thursday, 26th July
Anne, Mother of the Blessed Virgin Mary

Dear God,
Tom was called to the hospice at 6.15am to Anne James. Her father was already there. Tom anointed her and she died

at 7.10am, just as the hospice and the world were waking to a new day.

Audrey

Saturday 28th July

Dear God,

Major and Mrs Crabtree celebrated their Golden Wedding anniversary today. Their family, friends, Jessie their bridesmaid of fifty years ago, and Tom and I celebrated with them at their home this evening. It makes a nice change to meet people from outside the parish now and again.

But you know God, some people are quite thrown by a clerical collar. They either keep well away at the other side of the room, or form a little queue waiting to present their spiritual credentials. This evening was no exception.

First came Mr Pratt, a surveyor, who said he wasn't a great churchgoer, but was regular at Christmas and then disappeared with his drink to the far end of the room.

He was followed by Mrs Cooper, who said that her sister's husband's cousin's son was a priest in Norfolk with seven parishes and didn't Tom think that the Archbishop needed his head read to load seven parishes onto one man, while others with only one had nothing to do. At this point Tom accepted another whisky.

One of the grandsons was next. He'd done the atheist, the Buddhist and the Jesus bit, he said, and was now a humanist. He looked quite disappointed when Tom didn't challenge him, but asked him if he knew the latest cricket score.

Tom calls these the JIC (just in case) people who want to register their links with the church, no matter how tenuous, just in case it's all true.

The cake was a real work of art, provided by the publican's wife at the Dog and Duck in appreciation.

There were photographs on display of Major and Mrs

Crabtree's wedding in 1940. I could just about recognise the bride in white satin with her hair done up in bangs, but the major was unrecognisable. The Dog and Duck have a lot to answer for!

Tom and I enjoy these occasions immensely God. We feel privileged in sharing in these important milestones, these rites of passage.

Audrey

Sunday 29th July
Eighth Sunday after Pentecost
Theme: The Fruit of the Spirit

Dear God,

St Jude's Flower Festival ended today. It's been a great success and has attracted many people from outside our parish too.

Doris Stubbs was in her element and so was Primrose Flowers who'd done 'self control'. Her display generated much interest, but needed some explanation which she happily gave. 'The central lone white arum lily represents all that is pure and lovely,' she said. 'It's height and straightness symbolise steadfastness, integrity and strength of purpose. The uncontrolled profusion of sprigs of thorny Berberis and rambling red roses around its base symbolise all that distracts, ensnares and tests the self control of the traveller on the way.'

I'm glad that 'joy' can't be explained God.

Audrey

Wednesday 1st August
Lammas Day

Dear God,

Anne James was buried in St Jude's churchyard this afternoon. She'd been a faithful member of the Mothers' Union and their banner followed her coffin down the aisle.

Tom doesn't make long eulogies about the deceased, preferring to dwell more on the Christian hope of forgiveness and salvation. I did learn though that Anne had been a tireless worker for Amnesty International and had been supporting a child in Mozambique for the last five years. She never spoke about these things.

The sun came out as we all gathered round the reopened grave of Anne's mother for the committal and a reading from Revelation 14:13:

> And I heard a voice from heaven saying, 'Write this: Blessed are the dead who die in the Lord henceforth.' 'Blessed indeed,' says the Spirit, 'that they may rest from their labours, for their deeds follow them!'

Every time I go to a funeral God I'm very conscious of the fact that, no matter how insignificant the life of the deceased may have seemed to us, they now know what the rest of us don't.

Audrey

Thursday 2nd August

Dear God,

If another one of my sons dares to say, 'Relax Mum,' again, I'll go mad. Anthony even sports a T shirt with RELAX on it. But then he's not trying to keep five balls up in the air at once like me: the parish, three sons, a mother, a demonic dog and six hot flushes a minute.

I'm sure Tom was talking directly to me in the fifth pew last Sunday when he said, 'We've got to learn to "let go". Tension and worry will not solve ours or the world's problems; they will just block the channel in us through which the love of God flows out to others.'

I know he's right God, and I'm sure after our holiday in France I'll feel better. Do you think Anthony will lend me his T shirt for two weeks?

Only two more days God and we're off!

Audrey

Friday 3rd August

Dear God,

Mother moved into the rectory today to look after Martin, Sally and Pooky. Says she's going to get the garden into shape while we're away and bring some sense into Martin's room! I think she's looking forward to being in charge.

Derek left for his holiday job at Butlin's this morning and Anthony for Leigh Ann's daddy's gin palace on the Solent this afternoon.

Tom is horrified by the amount of luggage in the hall, but then he always is. He'd travel with only a carrier bag if he had his way. Anyway, I don't know what they've got or haven't got in France, do I God?

Audrey

Saturday 4th August
Dominic, Priest, Friar, 1221

Dear God,

We booked a cabin, but we got a cupboard. Tom is sleeping on the top shelf and I'm on the bottom. I've decided I'll be cremated, not buried, though I'm sure there's more headroom in a coffin. But God we've made it, we're on the ferry bound for Le Havre.

We arrived at Portsmouth ferry harbour at 7pm and by 8.30pm we were on board, with Josephine safely tucked away with all the other cars below deck.

Before ascending from the bowels of the ferry I had a joke with one of the officials. 'Don't forget to shut the doors,' I laughed. I was deadly serious God and Tom was dead embarrassed.

It was a balmy evening and we leant against the rails watching the lights of Portsmouth and the coastline recede into the distance.

About 10 o'clock, armed with the phrase *je voudrais* we headed for the restaurant to sample the cuisine. This turned out to be a choice between hamburgers or sausage, egg and chips. We were still a long way from French culinary delights.

I've been lying here now for two hours with sausage, egg and chips washed down with Coke lying heavily on my stomach. The world is gently rocking and oh God, I'M GOING TO BE SICK!

Audrey

Sunday 5th August
Ninth Sunday after Pentecost
Theme: The Whole Armour of God

Dear God,

I've crossed the English Channel. I'm on Gallic soil (which looks the same as British soil except it's dry).

We docked at Le Havre at 7.10am and at 7.40am were instructed to go to our cars. What a relief to be reunited with Josephine again, especially as she contained my entire summer wardrobe, my curling tongs and Tom's Sugar Puffs.

By 8 o'clock the cars were revving up ready to leave the ship. Ten minutes later Josephine hadn't moved and was receiving the last rites again. The cars behind hooted and the reverend used an expletive left over from his bad old rat-race days. Eventually we were pushed down the ramp and onto French soil.

Thus we were delivered into France and into a side lane so as not to impede the sleek automobiles behind as they roared past into Europe. I visualised us spending *Allez Dordogne* on the foreshore at Le Havre, while officials laughed at us in French. Then praise be! Josephine responded to another push start session and nine hours later we were in Siourac.

We located our gîte among a cluster of farmhouses and barns on a small hill. Below us lay fields of corn, sunflowers and the Dordogne river shimmering between groves of walnut trees.

The gîte's simple, almost spartan, and there's a mushroom growing in the corner of the loo. They seem to follow me God.

But I don't care. I don't care if Josephine never goes again. I don't care if she collapses into a heap on the driveway–we're here, I'M IN FRANCE, I'M ABROAD!

Audrey

Monday 6th August
The Transfiguration of Our Lord

Dear God,
 From French loos with no doors, Good Lord deliver me.
 From French loos with no seats, Good Lord deliver me.
 From French loos with a good view of other occupants,
Good Lord deliver me.
 One needs mega muscles to levitate in a sitting-up position
and not touch anything.
 After leaving the gîte in the morning we try not to drink;
just rinsing out our mouths with bottled *eau*. In Surlat we
gave way and gulped down some *café blanc* and spent the
whole afternoon holding on.

Audrey

Wednesday 8th August

Dear God,
 Under the sink in the gîte we've found enough cans of
spray and repellants to finish off the French ozone layer
completely, a whole armament against fleas, flies, ants, bees,
ticks and spiders.
 Talking of spiders God, all the French spiders decided to
spend the night at home last night, on the ceiling above our
bed and on the wall of the shower.
 One day I'll design a 'spider catcher' for all the arach-
nophobes like me. I'll make a fortune and we'll be able to
spend every summer in France.

Audrey

Thursday 9th August

Dear God,

The Dordogne churches – dust and artificial flowers every-where! Doris Stubbs would have a fit and the Holy Dusters would cry into their little orange squares.

But the mass of votive candles lit in hope, in faith, in thanksgiving, in petition and in pain, and the small Perrier bottles stuffed full of flowering wayside weeds at the foot of Mary gets to me God.

Audrey

Friday 10th August
Laurence, Deacon, Martyr, 258

Dear God,

Had lunch in Beynac today. Decided on *poisson* and chips after watching *l'homme* at the next table tucking into a pile of *escargots*.

I notice that children are welcome in restaurants. Also notice that between courses *le garçon* whips out the vacuum cleaner and clears the fall out around the *enfant*.

Audrey

Saturday 11th August
Clare of Assisi, Virgin, 1253

Dear God,

Sent Tom off for *deux baguette* this morning. Came back with *un baguette*. He'd forgotten the French for 'two' and did not want to risk putting up two fingers.

Oh God, the loo in the gîte is blocked up and we've been

so careful to follow all the instructions behind the loo door which end up by saying, 'IF YOU DO NOT FOLLOW THE ABOVE INSTRUCTIONS VERY CAREFULLY ALL THE STORIES YOU HAVE HEARD ABOUT FRENCH PLUMBING WILL COME TRUE!'

Audrey

Monday 13th August
Jeremy Taylor, Bishop of Down and Connor and Dromore, Pastor, Teacher, 1667

Dear God,

Madame Lauber, the landlady of the gîte, came round this morning. She's unilingual too, so there was much smiling and gesticulating. She brought us some of her homemade plum brandy.

This homemade brandy of Madame Lauber's is mentioned together with urgent warnings by previous tenants in the gîte's book of comments, and followed by at least four exclamation marks!!!!

It brought tears to our eyes so we poured it down the loo.

Audrey

Tuesday 14th August

Dear God,

Merci Dieu! The loo has miraculously unblocked itself overnight.

Audrey

Wednesday 15th August

Dear God,
  It's all so relaxing, suspended in time, cut off from news-papers, television and radio by the French language, no salmonella, no lysteria, no post, no phone calls, no heating systems, no wonky spires, no PCC meetings, no Doris Stubbs, no magazine, no souls to save, no 'greenhouse' effect, and NO MADGE DUNBAR!

Audrey

Thursday 16th August

Dear God,
  Today I tracked you down. You live in Rocamadour. I'll go back there one day to recapture the feeling of being halfway to heaven in the Nôtre Dame Chapel that's built into the rock face above the town which clings to the cliffs; where miracles happen, and I know they do.

Audrey

Friday 17th August

Dear God,
  Our last day and it's raining. Had a *petit* conversation with the nice man at the *supermarché* in Beynac. He pointed to the rain and said something about *Angleterre*. I wanted to say that actually *Angleterre* was having a drought at the moment, but had to settle for *oui* instead.
  Then, throwing caution to the winds, I ventured to say in two words that it was good for the flowers–*bon fleur*. The nice man then furthered the dialogue by knocking on the

counter to indicate that the ground was *très* hard. I came back bravely with, *oui*, and then went for the grand slam, describing everything as *très sec* (very dry)—a new word I'd learnt the night before from the wine bottle.

I should have left it at that God, grabbed my bottled *eau* and *pommes de terre*, and run. But it was all heady stuff and so I tried to say that we were leaving the next day.

The nice man, desperately trying to help, shouted, *'Voila'* and rushing over to the vegetables brought me back a bright orange pumpkin!

Audrey

Sunday 19th August
Eleventh Sunday after Pentecost
Theme: The Serving Community

Dear God,

Arrived back at the rectory last night at 11.30pm. Found a date loaf from Madge Dunbar in the porch, together with the August magazine.

Miss Willis popped round after breakfast with a bunch of flowers and to tell us that Mrs Hyde says she's not going to do the magazine anymore; Major Crabtree had slipped and broken his leg coming out of the Dog and Duck and was busy sueing the council for uneven surfaces; the Barber family (twenty-seven strong) had left St Jude's and were worshipping at the Methodist Church, because the rector had not been to see Nelly Barber when she'd had her legs done; the 'coffee morning' for a new church vacuum cleaner had raised £69.23, generously rounded up to £70 by Mrs Venn, and that Sister Perpetua had won the bottle of port.

Tom says there's no rest this side of the grave.

Audrey

Monday 20th August
Bernard, Abbot of Clairvaux, 1153

Dear God,

The gîte, the sunflowers, the walnut groves, the River Dordogne, the croissants and the sun faded today with six loads of washing and a visit to Tesco. But here are my five post holiday resolutions God: To spend more time in the garden and stop apologising for the weeds; to have a complete 'makeover' and throw away the remains of my No 7 make up; to try my hand at French cooking; to learn French, and to go back to France next year.

Audrey

Tuesday 21st August

Dear God,

Tom's first day back at work. He entered his study at 8.30am and sank without trace under a torrent of mail, ninety percent of it unsolicited. He surfaced at 5.30pm, ranting on about the trees that are being cut down and that when he retires he's sealing up his letter box.

Audrey

Sunday 26th August
Twelfth Sunday after Pentecost
Theme: The Witnessing Community

Dear God,

They were all there this morning at the 10.30am service, tanned and refreshed from their holidays and clutching a plethora of church magazines from Land's End to John O'Groats.

They were also armed with various solutions to St Jude's ills: from the church in Milton Keynes bursting at the seams with young people because they sing 'Onward Christian Soldiers' to the tune of *Neighbours*, to the church in Elgin where the rector and congregation wear T shirts exhorting the world to 'Be Saved at St Swithins'.

The collection bag this morning yielded up six pesetas and four centimes.

Audrey

Monday 27th August

Dear God,

I think Tom is suffering from post holiday blues. He says he wants to end his ministry in some forgotten country parish with a congregation of two: one with an impending heart attack and the other a rich widow who's willed all her money to the church roof, the organ and the heating system.

The trouble is God they've lumped all these clergy paradises together into benefices of three, four, five, six and even seven parishes.

Tom says his vision of hell is having seven Parochial Church Councils.

Audrey

Tuesday 28th August
Augustine, Bishop of Hippo, Teacher of the Faith, c 430

Dear God,

It's no easy task being a priest. As one priest describes it you can't win. If he visits he's nosey, if he doesn't he's a snob. If he preaches longer than ten minutes it's too long, if he preaches less than ten minutes he hasn't prepared his sermon. If he tells a joke he's flippant, if he doesn't he's far too serious. If he runs a bazaar he's money mad, if he doesn't there's no social life in the parish. If he's young he's inexperienced, if he's old he ought to retire.

But, when he dies there's never been anyone like him!

Audrey

Thursday 30th August

Dear God,
One year ago today Tom was inducted Rector of St Jude's. How has it gone God? There are no comforting guidelines like turnover or net profit. There's no bottom line to go by. 'Bums on seats' are sometimes confused with a priest's success and the spirituality of a church.

Maybe just to keep on keeping on is what a priest has to do God, as Tom's predecessor Father George, and his predecessor Father John, and all those previous rectors since 1407 whose names are listed on the wall of St Jude's did, endeavouring to carry out the charge given to them by their bishops at their ordinations.

Has Tom come up to St Jude's expectations? I expect not. Has he tried to do what his bishop charged him to do:

A priest is called by God to work with the bishop and with his fellow-priests, as servant and shepherd among the people to whom he is sent. He is to proclaim the word of the Lord, to call his hearers to repentance, and in Christ's name to absolve, and declare the forgiveness of sins. He is to baptize, and prepare the baptized for Confirmation. He is to preside at the celebration of the Holy Communion. He is to lead his people in prayer and worship, to intercede for them, to bless them in the name of the Lord, and to teach and encourage by word and example. He is to minister to the sick, and prepare the dying for their death. He must set the Good Shepherd always before him as the pattern of his calling, caring for the people committed to his charge, and joining with them in a common witness to the world.

He has tried.

I once heard a country parson say, 'I consider my job is to be the centre of prayer for my people', and I'm sure he's right God if, in that thought, he includes the bringing to his people the sacraments, especially the sacraments of Baptism, the Eucharist and Absolution.

For me it has been a steep learning curve. I wanted to do more than man the tea urn. I wanted to share with the people of St Jude's more than the amount of jumble coming in, or who won the two bottles of port.

I wanted to sweep them along with me in my own enthusiasm for books, ideas and discussion, but this was not to be. I've had to learn that we are not the author of each other's lives, but only companions on the way.

Instead I've been on the receiving end, sharing in and learning from their doubts, confusion and pain, and from their moments of joy too.

I've learnt about the diverse needs of your people. I've learnt, above all God, that you work in this world through people no matter how inadequate and flawed they may seem. I've seen your Holy Spirit working in their lives as they've tried, each in his own stumbling way, to be faithful to you.

I've learnt something of your peace and stillness on my visits to Polly Nightingale.

I've seen the particular pain of those who cannot accept you God, yet want a Christian burial.

I've learnt of the invincibility of the human spirit when I've visited the terminally ill and found them nurturing seeds on their kitchen window sill.

I've learnt of the warmth and strength of being where others are gathered in prayer. I've learnt about waiting on you.

God, whatever this year has meant for the worshippers of St Jude's, it has been a growing period for me.

What of the boys? How has it been for them? Have they only heard of the difficulties, uncertainties, frustrations and irritations of their father's new career? Have they only heard of the Doris Stubbs and Madge Dunbars in the church, and not of the Polly Nightingales and of those who grow seedlings which they won't live to plant out?

Has their close encounter with the church this year helped or hindered them? Will they one day make Christianity their own through conviction, instead of nominally through inheritance? Will they be able to make that leap across in faith with all the baggage of doubts and uncertainties on their backs we all share?

God, my prayer for them lies in the last lines of the prayer of St Richard of Chichester, slightly paraphrased:

> May they know thee more clearly
> May they love thee more dearly
> May they follow thee more nearly.

Audrey

Friday 31st August
Aidan, Bishop of Lindisfarne, Missionary, 651
John Bunyan, Author, 1688

Dear God,

I hope that before I die I am able to make my confession and receive absolution. I'd like my coffin to rest in church overnight.

At the start of the funeral service the priest will come up the aisle saying: Jesus said, 'I am the resurrection and the life; he who believes in me, though he die, yet shall he live, and whoever lives and believes in me shall never die' (Jn 11:25-26).

I would like the reading from Revelation 21:1-7:

> Then I saw a new heaven and a new earth; for the first heaven and the first earth had passed away, and the sea was no more. And I saw the holy city, new Jerusalem, coming down out of heaven from God, prepared as a bride adorned for her husband; and I heard a loud voice from the throne saying, 'Behold, the dwelling of God is with men...He who conquers shall have this heritage, and I will be his God and he shall be my son.

You know God how much I have loved hymns. You know how they've comforted, calmed, humbled, lifted, thrilled and inspired me throughout my life, and you know how difficult it is for me to choose from them now for my funeral, but here they are:

(1) 'Praise my soul the King of Heaven', which was my school hymn and which accompanied me down the aisle to marry my beloved Tom.

(2) 'Dear Lord and Father of Mankind', especially for the phrase 'forgive our foolish ways'.

(3) 'Abide with me' for the lines 'Hold thou thy cross before my closing eyes; Shine through the gloom, and point me to the skies'. I wish that it could be so for me.

(4) 'The Day thou gavest Lord is ended' which I sang at my Father's funeral.

The address would be about Christian hope.

Before the blessing the priest will read the *Nunc Dimittis*:

> Lord, now lettest thou thy servant depart in peace: according to thy word,
> For mine eyes have seen: thy salvation;
> Which thou hast prepared: before the face of all people;

To be a light to lighten the Gentiles: and to be the glory of thy people Israel.

And lastly God, as they pick up my coffin and turn to go down the aisle, the organ will pound out the last hymn, 'Thine be the glory', because God, if I ever get near the pearly gates, it will not be because of what I've done, but because of your mercy and forgiveness.

Then, as the last strains of the organ die away, everyone may repair to the hall and tuck into the sandwiches, iced cupcakes and cold sausage rolls that stick to the roof of your mouth.

Now dear God before I go to sleep tonight here is the third collect for Tom, for Derek, for Anthony, for Martin, for Mother, for Sally, for Pooky and for all the people of St Jude's:

Lighten our darkness, we beseech thee, O Lord; and by thy great mercy defend us from all perils and dangers of this night; for the love of thy only Son, our Saviour, Jesus Christ. Amen.